2-IN-1 VA

SAVE
MONEY
AND
WORK
FROM
HOME

DURING AND AFTER
THE ECONOMIC CRISIS

Personal Finance, Managing Money, Online Freelance
and Entrepreneurship Tips For Difficult Times

DANA WISE

2-IN-1 VALUE

SAVE MONEY
AND
WORK
FROM
HOME

DURING AND AFTER
THE ECONOMIC CRISIS

Personal Finance, Managing Money, Online Freelance
and Entrepreneurship Tips For Difficult Times

DANA WISE

2020

Table of Contents

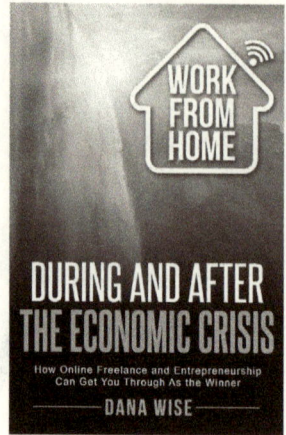

SAVE
MONEY
AND
SPEND
WISELY

TWO VALUABLE FORMS

WORK FROM HOME CHECKLIST
Top ten tips for your daily productivity

- ☑ The selection from 23 tips for working from home described in the book
- ☑ Daily habits for the most effective remote work
- ☑ Must have for a productive freelancer or entrepreneur

I will save on
Your one-page saving form

	DONE
Actions and SMART goals that you will achieve	✓
Maximize your immediate saving	✓
Save many thousands every year	✓
BONUS: non-financial benefits for your dream life	✓

To download your checklist, click and visit the link:

rsagile.activehosted.com/f/11

WORK FROM HOME

DURING AND AFTER THE ECONOMIC CRISIS

How Online Freelance and Entrepreneurship
Can Get You Through As the Winner

DANA WISE

INTRODUCTION

WE live in frightening times with this recent coronavirus pandemic affecting every person on this planet, and it's even worse if you're one of the millions of people who can't afford to miss a paycheck. If you have some money saved up, that may not last as long as the crisis. The exact economic impact of the pandemic hasn't been evaluated fully yet, but estimates have ranged anywhere from 6% to 20% unemployment.

The uncertainty is a big part of the problem, as the stock market has been fluctuating wildly while the world struggles to respond to the pandemic. While experts believe the markets might rebound after the crisis passes, it may be too late for many investors, along with the workers employed by companies reliant on those investors. The coronavirus may be creating the deepest and fastest economic crisis since before World War II. There is bad news everywhere you turn, but remember that the worst thing you can do is panic. Therefore, what exactly *should* you do to save yourself from economic ruin?

It may be time to rearrange our thinking about how and where we work. Some bright spots might emerge as a result of this crisis. This book will present quick and effective solutions to the problem of finding work while practicing social distancing.

You can make money quickly while isolated at home, and the following suggestions can ultimately be long-term. Even after restrictions are lifted, it will take a long time for life to return to normal.

Post-coronavirus life may be very different from what we're used to today. Those changes represent an enormous opportunity for online businesses and freelance work, which is what this book is about. This book will present information about a variety of online businesses and freelancing opportunities.

Here are a few things we know about the current crisis and
online work:

- Online work is one of the fastest growing business opportunities during the current crisis.

- It is likely to remain in very high demand, even after the crisis passes and the economy returns to normal.

- The post-coronavirus world will probably become quite different, since many companies will have likely transformed themselves; they will be far more willing to work with freelancers and startup online businesses.

This presents the best opportunity for those who are willing to engage in a new way of doing business.

If you want to be a winner and not a victim in this crisis, continue reading, as this book will change your life. It will help you explore a new way to work that will allow you more flexibility in your schedule and lifestyle. It's the perfect solution for the current crisis that can give you a competitive advantage, even after the crisis has passed. More than 4.7 million people—approximately 3.4% of the population—are currently working remotely, and that successful trend has been steadily growing within the last few years[1] (Braccio-Hering, 2020). When you include the number of people doing freelance work part-time, that figure rises to a whopping 57 million—or 34%—in the United States alone[2] (Upwork, 2019). This crisis has presented a major opportunity to jump into the remote workforce and refocus our business aspirations.

But, can you get started? Well, that is what this book will be discussing. I'll take you through the various types of opportunities available in online work and show you how to get started. We will be looking at freelance work and entrepreneurial or small business opportunities and discussing the types of work available in these various fields, required qualifications and experience, preferred jobs, trends in online entrepreneurship, and how you can build your brand online. While previous crises have meant the end of many businesses, the current one does present an opportunity 13 for YOU to create a flexible business model and become a leader in the online business world. But why am I the one who can help you do this? Let me tell you a little about myself and my own online transformation.

Prior to going online, I was working for several larger companies. My manager was challenging me to treat my department as if it were my own company. Specifically, he wanted me to save on expenses, bring innovations, improve processes, and, generally, have an entrepreneurial mindset. I agreed with him but found it difficult to make any real changes. Maybe I was too deep in the corporate mindset—that is, I was too worried about securing my workplace and defending against risks. In any case, it wasn't working out, so I made the leap to create my own business and go remote.

Therefore, I can say that I fully understand your situation; however, you have two advantages that I did not have—one is the current crisis pushing people to stay at home and giving them time to think carefully about important things. The second advantage you have is me, and I've done what I'm about to describe to you. I know what it takes to make the change successfully, and I will take you through the process, highlight what you need to consider, and show you how to get your new lifestyle up and running.

You may think you are too shy and not assertive enough to go through the challenges this will require. I was thinking the same about myself, and it took me over a year to find my way. Another challenge I faced was that I thought I was not creative enough. I wondered what I would do, what value would I give my customers, how could I find them, and how could I make enough earnings to survive? The perspective I needed came from a friend of mine. That friend made me realize that it doesn't matter what your nature is—it only matters whether you're willing to take the risk.

It's just a matter of time until you start seeing results.

I will show you how I worked everything out and how you can too. Currently, I am working five different freelancing and entrepreneur jobs—some local and some remote. I was also affected by the coronavirus crisis, but that has only proved to me how valuable it is to have built a remote business. I had to suspend some of my local onsite jobs, but because of my remote work capabilities, I am now able to continue working without disruption to my income. Since I cannot clone myself, I had to reduce some streams and prioritize others. I have made it work, and I want to show you how you can make it work too.

Working online requires a change in perspective, but these opportunities have been growing since before the pandemic. There are now even more possibilities with the global pandemic forces radically changing their lives. Consider this your opportunity to take your life into your own hands and create the future you've always dreamed about—one where you control your schedule, your talents can shine, and you can help both yourself and your loved ones navigate this brave new world.

There's no better time than right now to make the changes that will give you the freedom to do what you love and change your life for the better, while at the same time staying safe and healthy during the current crisis. This book will guide you through the many ways you can meet the challenge of this crisis and not only survive, but thrive!

Today is a great day to create your future, so let's get started!

---

[1] https://www.flexjobs.com/blog/post/remote-work-statistics/
[2] https://www.upwork.com/press/2019/10/03/freelancing-in-america-2019/

Chapter **ONE**

UNDERSTANDING THE THREAT OF CORONAVIRUS TO YOUR PHYSICAL AND ECONOMIC WELL-BEING

THE novel coronavirus has presented a different threat compared to what we've seen in recent years. But where did it come from, and how does it spread? It's important to understand the coronavirus to comprehend the nature of both the health and economic threat it poses in full. For that reason, I will be spending a little time discussing the origin, symptoms, health impacts, mortality rate, and economic impacts of the pandemic. It's essential to remain informed about the situation, so we can make the best decisions.

While much of the information about the coronavirus has been negative, this book will help you make positive changes to meet the challenges brought on by this pandemic. There are things you can do and control, and there is a way out of these difficult times; however, understanding the facts is key to finding a way forward. It's also important to gain as much knowledge of this experience as possible to facilitate planning for future crises. Let's start by taking a look at the origins and nature of the coronavirus.

Coronavirus and Its Origins

There are actually various forms of coronavirus, and they are all responsible for a range of illnesses—from the common cold to more severe diseases such as Middle East Respiratory Syndrome (MERS) and Severe Acute Respiratory Syndrome (SARS). The current pandemic is caused by a new strain of coronavirus, which causes an illness known as **COVID-19**. Until now, this strain was yet to be observed in humans.

Coronaviruses, along with this new one, are what are called **zoonotic diseases**, meaning they are transmitted between animals and humans. For example, SARS was originally transmitted from civet cats to humans, and MERS was transmitted from dromedary camels to humans. The current coronavirus is speculated to have originated in one of two species—bats and/or pangolins (an armadillo-like animal found in Asia and Africa).

Zoonotic diseases are common, and when you think about it from an evolutionary standpoint, it makes sense. When two species are in close contact—as with humans and animals—the virus has an opportunity to mutate and adapt to the other species, thus allowing it to have more hosts. When you're around an animal frequently, you would also be exposed to any pathogens that infect that animal—however, if that pathogen gets into you during this stage, it can't infect you. As it passes through your system often from frequent exposure, it—like any organism in a new environment—adapts. As it adapts and mutates, that is when it becomes able to infect you.

We've been around our domestic animals for thousands of years, so we've already adapted to their pathogens and they to ours; however, we haven't been exposed in the same way to those of wild animals. These animals represent a whole new reservoir of disease, making wild animal markets, such as the one in Wuhan, China, very dangerous.

19

Coronavirus Symptoms

The current coronavirus, which causes COVID-19, attacks the respiratory system; therefore, common symptoms include fever, cough, shortness of breath, and breathing difficulties. In severe cases, it can cause pneumonia, SARS, kidney failure, and even potentially death. The recommendations to prevent infection are one of the reasons for the social distancing, which is the primary cause of various problems in our global economy. The preventative recommendations include the following:

- Wash your hands regularly for at least 20 seconds.
- Cover your mouth and nose when coughing and/or sneezing.
- Use a protective mask and gloves when going outside.
- Cooking meat and eggs thoroughly.
- Avoid close contact with other people (social distancing).
- Avoid touching your mouth, nose, and eyes.
- Stay home if you have symptoms.
- Clean surfaces and objects that you touch regularly, such as your kitchen counter, credit card, and keys.

While people with symptoms may be the most contagious, health officials now believe that asymptomatic people may be responsible for more transmission than previously thought. That is partially why it's been so difficult for officials to get the spread of the infection under control. In addition, many people only experience mild symptoms, but they are still highly contagious[3] (Cohen, 2020).

Another factor that complicates the picture is how long coronavirus can live on surfaces. Researchers so far have observed that one strain of coronavirus can live for several hours to even days in aerosols and on surfaces. In addition, scientists at the National

Institutes of Health (NIH), the Centers for Disease Control and Prevention (CDC), the University of California, Los Angeles (UCLA), and Princeton University have all found that this new coronavirus, dubbed **SARS-CoV-2**, was detectable in aerosols for up to three hours, on copper for up to four hours, on cardboard for up to 24 hours, and on plastic and stainless steel for up to three days. Their studies have shown that, although the virus isn't naturally airborne, it can stay in the air and on droplets for several hours, and people can contract the virus after touching contaminated surfaces, even if it has been sitting on the same materials for a few days[4] (van Doremalen et al., 2020).

Coronavirus Mortality Rate

The mortality rate is another important consideration related to the novel coronavirus. Part of the problem with determining the mortality rate is that insufficient testing and mild symptoms in many people could mean that the rate of those infected has been seriously underestimated. As of this writing (March 31th, 2020), there have been 858,319 confirmed cases of coronavirus and 42,302 deaths worldwide. Taken at face value, that's a mortality rate of approximately 4%, but assessing the death rate is much more complex than that, in part because there may actually be thousands of infected people out there who have not been tested. The World Health Organization (WHO) estimates the fatality rate at 3.4%. Most experts agree that the novel coronavirus likely has a higher mortality rate than the seasonal flu, but they also believe it is not as high as what WHO estimates because of the unreported cases.

Still, regardless of the mortality rate, the proper restrictions are now in place to protect a large portion of the population. By flattening the curve of cases, the hospitals can then deal with more incoming patients. If too many infected people flood the hospitals 21 all at once, the hospitals will be overwhelmed. Thus, the isolation and stay-at-home orders help prevent that from happening. That's why it's important that you follow the health and recommendations put forth by authorities, researchers, and WHO. Nonetheless, for all of us, there also exist economic problems. We will be taking a look at that.

The Economic Impact of Coronavirus

Given the rapid spread of coronavirus, the response from governments, businesses, and families has been variable, albeit massive and disruptive to the economy, both local and global. Though the steps taken by policymakers are necessary, the changes will have a ripple effect throughout every level of society. Here are the facts as of March of 2020:

- Though the economic markets are reacting wildly to the crisis, it has slowed down due to the global pandemic—not some core economic weakness. The economic impact of the virus is still highly unpredictable.

- The pandemic will affect all countries and almost all industries, and it has already disrupted supply chains, such as manufacturing plants that are now sitting idle. Understandably, warehouse workers are either becoming ill or staying home not to get the disease.

- The severity of the disease necessitates that the population's health and safety is the highest priority. While governments are seeking to ensure they have sufficient diagnostic, protective, and therapeutic equipment available, policymakers still need to ensure that economically vulnerable workers—in the healthcare industry and beyond—do not have to choose between working while sick and staying home. To do that, they need to make sure that workers have access to paid sick leave, paid medical leave, and family leave. That means they will need to expand current protections to enable those who are self-employed to also receive benefits.

◻ Demand is hurting more than supply; in other words, most economic disruptions have mainly impacted the demand side of the economic equation. As people are unable to go to work, they risk losing their jobs and incomes as businesses are forced to close. Additionally, businesses have had to put investments on hold amid the growing uncertainty.

◻ Exports will likely falter as countries around the world are forced to take similar actions to slow the spread of the disease.

What are Policymakers Planning to Do?

There are a number of proposals that policymakers are considering to assist with the economic impact. The main problem faced by businesses is the lack of customers and sustainable cash income that can last them for an extended period of time. That means small and medium-sized businesses will feel the impact first and more severely. Thus, economic interventions need to focus on boosting demand within the economic equation. That will likely mean replacing incomes, particularly in low and middle income families, who will be less likely to have sufficient savings to see them through the crisis.

Policymakers will, however, also have to watch and support the supply side of the economy, particularly for those businesses that are and have been hard hit by the loss of demand, like the travel and tourism industries. Uncertainty is only exacerbating the situation as businesses are reacting to not knowing how much worse it can get. Families are doing the same—they are cutting spending in fear that they will face a drastic drop in income. That's where the federal government can act to help address the 23 uncertainty. First and foremost, Congress and the President need to be clear that they will be undertaking the necessary steps to stop an economic freefall.

Because state and local governments are on the frontline of the crisis, they need sufficient fiscal support from the federal government for securing what they need to supply public services required in their communities and support local businesses threatened by the pandemic. A factor within those communities is economic inequality, which is a problem highlighted by the current pandemic.

Income and wealth inequality create vicious cycles for lower income families. These families have lower pay; less in their savings; and fewer benefits, like health insurance and paid sick leave; to rely on during this crisis. That means they face a higher risk of infection, loss of income, along with massive health care bills. Thus, policymakers are trying to enact a number of policies to assist workers within these families. These policies include instituting moratoriums on student debt, car loans, and credit card payments.

Though the stock market has been fluctuating like crazy since the pandemic began, the focus of these policymakers need to remain on the most vulnerable in society rather than the Wall Street investors. Most people don't own stocks on Wall Street or in any other national market; thus, the ups and downs there have little impact on their personal financial health. For that reason, policymakers are negotiating cash infusions to every American, though the exact amount and timing has yet to be determined as of this writing (March 2020).

Finally, this crisis has also served to demonstrate the limit of the Federal Reserve in attacking such economic crises. While the federal government has cut interest rates aggressively to zero, those

will have little effect on the economy in the short-term. The interest rates for mortgages and business loans were already low, and other interest rates, such as those for student and car loans and credit cards, have been notoriously impervious to changes in the federal funds rate.

Adding to this is how most businesses are not yet hurting for capital to invest. Tax cuts aimed at large corporations don't have the trickle down effect that policymakers might have intended, and with the last tax cut, companies simply decided not to invest the money. Therefore, any interest rate cuts will likely do little to stimulate business investment.

Help Yourself

At the moment, all any business can do is wait for the decisions of fiscal policymakers and see if these changes will help the situation. However, that might not be good enough for most workers, so what exactly can you do to help yourself? Of course, you should first make sure you are complying with the health recommendations of the experts at the CDC and your local medical centers. Getting sick will only exacerbate any economic problems you might already be experiencing as a result of the coronavirus pandemic.

If you or your family need to start saving large amounts immediately, I would recommend that you read my other book *Save Money and Spend Wisely During and After the Economic Crisis*. You will discover many other tips about reducing your spending instantly, helping you save money over the coming weeks and months while this crisis lasts.

Economically, however, there may be more things you can do than simply sitting in isolation at home. You can remain isolated while still taking advantage of the growing online business opportunities that will likely become more mainstream as this crisis evolves.

We will examine those opportunities for you in subsequent chapters.

Chapter Summary

In this chapter, we discussed the physical and economic impacts of the coronavirus pandemic. Specifically, we discussed the following topics:

- Coronavirus and its origins.
- Coronavirus symptoms.
- The coronavirus mortality rate.
- The economic impact of coronavirus.
- What policymakers are planning.
- How these facts can help you make the right decisions going forward.

In the next chapter, I will be showing you the general types of remote work you can do and some practical tips for working from home successfully.

---

[3] https://edition.cnn.com/2020/03/14/health/coronavirus-asymptomatic-spread/index.html

[4] Aerosol and Surface Stability of SARS-CoV-2 as Compared with SARS-CoV-1. *New England Journal of Medicine.* https://doi.org/10.1056/nejmc2004973

Chapter TWO

WORK FROM HOME STRATEGIES

THERE are a couple different strategies you can employ when working remotely, and you will want to explore the options that will suit your personal preferences and situation the best. It's worthwhile to review the different strategies and tips for working from home. It does require a heightened degree of self-motivation and control, as well as the need to put strong boundaries in place between your work and personal life. Let's take a look at some options and strategies for working from home.

Work from Home Options

You might not have the slightest idea of what kind of work you can do from home, but by looking at the most popular work-from-home job options, you can have a better idea of the variety of jobs that can be done remotely. Let's look at a list of the 23 most popular remote job titles as of October, 2019[5] (Howington, 2019):

Internal Services

- *Bookkeeper*—this work involves processing documents, posting entries, keeping order, preparing invoices, handling accounts receivable and payable, along with other admin tasks.

- *Accountant*—this involves analyzing books and turning that data into useful information, setting financial data structures, and helping with financial matters like preparing tax returns.

- *Engineer*—there are many kinds of engineers, such as mechanical, civil, chemical, electrical, computer, and software. Engineers use science, math, and technology to solve various problems, much of which can be done remotely. This fact is particularly true for computer/software engineers.

- *Project manager*—project managers help keep projects on track to achieve the required milestones. They also help track budgets and deadlines, delegate duties, and ensure that deliverables are completed on time. Their work is critical but does not necessarily have to be conducted in person.

- *Program manager*—program managers oversee tasks and projects that help companies achieve their business objectives. It is similar to project management, but usually involves overseeing related projects. Project managers help implement strategies and calculate the return on investment for programs and projects. It's an area of work that can easily be done remotely.

- *Interim/part-time manager*—this job requires working between 10 to 30 hours a week as a manager/leader, or during a vacancy period when the client needs to cover daily work before finding a permanent employee. These jobs may also be required to help with busy projects or during times of fast growth when the client needs to cover tasks temporarily.

- *Recruiter*—these people look for qualified candidates for job openings. They often write and post job descriptions, network, interview candidates, onboard new employees, and help maintain the company culture. They also approach freelancers and interim managers when the client needs those services.

Advisory and Education

- *Education*—online education has been becoming increasingly more popular over the years, and it is expected that the market will continue growing quickly. It is a successful strategy for many subject areas—teachers, tutors, and coaches can easily make use of established online educational platforms for working with students in groups or one-on-one settings.

- *Consultant*—consultants work to help companies, organizations, and individuals solve problems, find areas for improvement, and finish projects. They are individuals with expertise and experience in their field. However, for many businesses and educational fields, healthcare industries, and IT companies, consultants are a valuable part of the workforce, and they are able to do much, if not all, of their work remotely.

- *Business development manager*—business development managers can help find new business opportunities for increasing revenue. They do this by writing proposals, finding sales leads, and making sales pitches. The role requires mainly communication capabilities and networking skills. Knowledge of online marketing tools and techniques will give a greater advantage when looking for work in this field.

- *Data analyst*—this job entails interpreting various data to assist companies while they make business decisions. As part of that work, the data analyst will collect information and evaluate it for patterns. They will then compile their findings and draft reports for the company to use in the decision-making and problem-solving process.

High Demand Services

◻ *Writer*—this is one of the most common remote jobs. There are many mediums and subjects for which writers can create content, including articles, books, blog posts, emails, ad copy, and technical manuals. There are numerous online websites, newspapers, magazines, blogs, and companies that are willing to pay well for great content.

◻ *Editor*—this job entails correcting errors within written content. Editors rewrite content frequently to make it clearer, and they may also pitch ideas, provide feedback to writers, and write headlines.

◻ *UX/UI designer*—this involves facilitating the user experience and interface of a product. These individuals often create flowcharts, produce codes and scripts, and design prototyping concepts. This is another popular remote job.

◻ *Web developer*—web developers create attractive and functional websites, using their coding and graphic design skills to do so. This job usually requires expertise in HTML, CSS, JavaScript, jQuery, APIs, and frameworks built on the languages. You can work as a web developer completely from home, and there is an extremely high demand for skilled developers.

◻ *Programmers*—programmers use computer coding languages to write software and create mobile applications and websites. This is another popular remote job.

Sales and Marketing

◻ *Customer service representative*—customer service representatives are people who focus on helping customers or clients. They do this by using telephones, email, online chats, or social media to help answer questions, place orders, and resolve customer problems.

31

- *Sales representative*—these individuals sell products and services, and they also often deliver presentations and demonstrations, participate in sales meetings, and keep up-to-date on product information. Much of this work can be done remotely.

- *Account manager/account executive*—these individuals oversee client relations. They help generate sales by upselling, cross-selling, maintaining positive client relationships, and handling client communications. This is a very common remote job.

- *Territory sales manager*—this job entails developing sales prospects, creating sales strategies, maintaining customer relationships, and meeting sales goals. This is a popular remote job and is assigned typically to specific regions or territories. It also often requires travel.

Healthcare

- *Medical coder*—this job involves assigning codes to diagnoses and procedures listed on medical charts and performed on patients. People who work in this field usually work for hospitals, clinics, and/or physician's offices, but it is common for the work itself to be done remotely.

- *Nurse*—while nurses have been in demand even before the current pandemic, it is now a job that can be done remotely via telehealth platforms. This job typically requires providing assistance to patients through phone messaging, video conferencing, messaging, and/or emailing. Usually, these nurses are answering questions, instructing patients on treatments, and/or providing medical advice.

- *Case manager*—this job entails assessing patient needs, then helping find resources that they require. It can include advocating for patients, providing guidance and/or education, and building relationships with patients and their families.

This list of available remote opportunities is by no means exhaustive—these are just some of the more popular remote jobs. Other options include becoming a virtual assistant, data entry technician, administration, among other titles. Some remote jobs require education and experience, but others are entry-level with minimal requirements. There are truly many opportunities, and any sector will offer a broad range of specific jobs with countless opportunities, many of which will likely match your talents, skills, experience, and preferences.

The type of work you might be able to do will depend on your personal situation, but there is a niche among the possibilities regardless of your level of education or experience. Aside from these remote employee positions, there is also the opportunity to create your own business to meet your increasing needs. We will be discussing both freelance work and business creation in the chapters to come, but for now, we will be taking a look at a few tips from people who are successfully working from home now and how they do it.

23 Tips for Working from Home

Working from home requires a different mindset compared to otherwise because it's easy to get distracted by the familiarity of the home environment. It's also easy to procrastinate and convince yourself that you'll just work later. It is easy to procrastinate because there is no boss to tell you what to do on that specific day. That's why these tips from the people who have been successful in working from home can help set yourself up for success.

1. *Set regular work hours—even if that means at night.* You have to do what works for you, but setting specific and consistent work hours and beginning your day early will help motivate you to work. Even if you're a night owl and you plan to work at night, treat it like you would do a job to which you have to commute. **33**

Get yourself ready for work, then "go" to your office like you would with any other job.

TIP: *Write and print your schedule that will contain blocks of requirements (e.g. bring children to school), work, breaks, and other activities. Having your schedule in front of you makes the most efficient use of your time.*

2. **Get started early.** Working early will help you set the tone for your day and feel ready to work. This also applies even if your "morning" is at 9 PM. Some successful remote workers even put off their first meal of the day until during their first break of the day.

TIP: *Schedule your morning by allocating specific amounts of time for your routine prior to work (e.g., 8:00-8:30: showering and brushing teeth). Stick to that schedule so you can get to working as quickly as possible.*

3. **Dedicate a space as your office.** You really need to create a separation between your work and home life, and by dedicating a space as your office, you will accomplish that. You will also become accustomed to thinking of that space as the place to get down to business rather than for other leisure activities. Even if your "office" consists of a folding table and chair, it's actually the mental perception that matters. You will come to see that area as your office and associate it with work rather than play.

TIP: *If you have a dedicated home office space, put the name of your company on the door to make it look and feel as official as possible.*

4. **Treat your office as if it was a real office.** This means that you would do all the things you normally would if you were going into the office. In other words, you get up and go through your normal morning routine—shower, shave, eat breakfast, and dress for the office—and then you go to your office. The only difference should be that you have a shorter commute. Treating

work at home the same as an office will really get you into the proper frame of mind for working, which will then help you be more productive.

5. *Structure your day just like you would at the office.* When you're working from home, it will be easier to lose focus, put things off, or burn out. To prevent that, determine exactly what you need to do for the day and when you will accomplish those tasks. Use a calendar, computer program, or cell phone to schedule events and set reminders for yourself. Use the same schedule you would in the office—so, if you would normally respond to emails first thing at the office, then do the same in your home office. That will help keep you in the right mindset for work.

6. *Make it difficult to mess around on social media.* You don't want to get lost in reading through your social media, which is easy to do. To prevent that possibility, it may be a good idea to remove the social media shortcuts from your work computer or log out of your accounts. Doing so will make it harder to quickly check-in. It's also a good idea to try working in "incognito," "unavailable," or "private" mode, or whatever other mode your browser has that will tell people you're not currently available.

People on social media do not respect the need for privacy, and they often expect an immediate response. However, in this case, you are at work building your and your family's future; therefore, you need to ensure you get the privacy you need. You will need to respect your goals. The same rules apply to your private email. Remember—you're at work, and you can't browse social media if you want to get your work done, whether that is at the office or at home.

TIP: You can turn social media on in the afternoon break for the first time, quickly respond, and close them until evening.

7. ***Create boundaries for family members.*** Just like you, your family members or roommates who might be at home while you're working need to realize that you're working. They can't just walk into your office and disturb your flow. Make it clear that, just like at the office, they need to knock on the door and ask if it's a good time for you. If you don't set the boundaries, it will be easy for them to interrupt your work, and it will also be easy for you to get distracted. They need to understand that, just because you're working from home, it doesn't mean that you're home and available for responding to their needs. If you don't have an office door, use another signal—like headphones— to indicate to your family that you're busy.

   TIP: *Keep the door closed and put your schedule on it for family members. Agree with your family that you need to focus 100%, but during breaks, you can 100% be with them.*

8. ***Rent an office.*** For some people, it may not be possible to create an office for various reasons. Therefore, it may be a good option to rent an office nearby. You can have a shared office space with other like-minded people, which will also allow you to encourage each other when working on achieving your goals.

9. ***Work when you're most productive.*** Your motivation and energy levels will naturally ebb and flow throughout the day. Therefore, try to recognize your normal rhythms and use that knowledge to work when you know you have the energy to get more done. Save harder tasks for the time of day when you know you're at your best while saving the easier work for when you know you typically drag a little.

   Many people are most productive from early morning until lunchtime. If that's you, schedule the most important tasks for the morning. Then, designate the early afternoon to downtime, and it may ultimately be more productive to take a longer break—like a siesta. Then, after 2 or 3 pm, productivity typically increases and reaches a peak that lasts until about 6 pm. Our brain goes into a sleep mode in the night, then it will only reach about a half or third of its peak productivity compared to the morning peak.

10. *Take clear breaks.* This is important, because it's so easy to just blast through your day without stopping. However, research has shown that those who work with frequent breaks are actually more productive than those who just put their head down and work until the task is done. In fact, researchers have found that the ideal work rhythm is 52 minutes of work followed by a 17-minute break. In this study, workers remained completely dedicated to the task at hand for about an hour, but then, once they took a break, they felt refreshed and ready to dive back in for another productive hour of work[6] (Zetlin, 2020).

Additionally, there's a neurological reason for why this works. The brain works naturally in bursts of high activity for approximately one hour; after that length of time, it will switch to low activity for a while. That's when you should take a break. If you don't, your productivity will suffer. Although the research shows that if you take more breaks, your productivity will likely be reduced about once every hour, your productivity is still higher than those who work longer with no breaks. Furthermore, it's critical that you really take that break. That means disconnecting from work, getting up from your desk, and walking away from your computer. In fact, taking a walk is a great and effective way to take a break (Zetlin, 2020). And, definitely do not sit at the computer for an extended period of time.

11. *Set a time for your workday to end.* When you're working from home, it's easy to keep going, especially if you really wanted to get that task done. However, just like any other job, your workday should have a definite end time. Of course, sometimes it is necessary to work overtime, but that should be the *exception*—not the rule. Not doing so can result in burnout.

12. ***Commit to doing more.*** It's a great idea to overestimate how much time you'll spend doing one task, as most projects often take more time than you initially thought they would. By overestimating the length of time you'll need, you will feel more productive when you get things done more quickly. Even if you don't quite finish all the tasks you wanted to get done, you will still come out ahead after having completed a solid list of tasks. This technique can help keep you honest.

13. ***Make calls when you're alert and ready to interact socially.*** For some people, this may mean waiting until later in the day to make phone calls; however, others may feel fresher in the morning. Whatever is the case in your situation, arrange a time for making calls and other mentally challenging tasks when you feel most alert.

    If you do not need your phone for work, it's best to just turn it off completely. Even an SMS will draw your attention and distract you, and once you've broken your attention away from your work, it will take you several minutes or even hours for your brain to refocus and get back to top-level productivity. If you cannot turn your phone off, put it on silent and place it in another room. You can check it during breaks and return any important calls before you get back to work.

14. ***Focus on one task at a time.*** There's a popular misconception that multitasking increases productivity; however, the research on this specific topic says otherwise. Stanford researchers Uncapher and Wagner[7] (2018) found that heavy multitaskers performed worse than those who focused on one thing at a time. The researchers speculated the reason was because they experienced problems when organizing their thoughts and filtering out irrelevant information. The participants were also slower at switching from one task to another. Thus, the studies suggest that you'll be more productive if you work on one task at a time.

15. *Plan your week ahead of time.* This will reduce the amount of time you spend each day on planning. Of course, you can change your agenda if needed, but if you can commit to an agenda ahead of time, you will feel more organized and ready to go each day.

16. *Plan tomorrow—today.* Similar to the last task, you should plan tasks and activities for the next working day on your schedule. *Be specific*—it will help you start working on a particular task from the first minute as soon as you get into the office.

17. *Use technology to stay connected.* For online work, this is a *must.* There are various forms of technologies that will let you stay in touch with clients or coworkers. Programs like Zoom, Google Hangouts, Slack, and Skype make teleconferencing easy, and there's always instant messaging to communicate quickly. Be sure you have all the tools you need installed before you get started, so you don't have to deal with downloading and installing a program before you can reach out.

    TIP: *Create accounts with your business address; therefore, you will have a place where you will have only business contacts without being disrupted by friends.*

18. *Use music or other background noises to keep you motivated while working.* Some people like to work to music. If that's you, make sure the music suits the task at hand or is audio that won't distract you. Download your playlists ahead of time and line them up so you won't have to continue looking for songs to add to your soundtrack. If the music you are listening to is distracting (which is also my case), a good option is to have noise that will prevent other distracting sounds. You can find noise broadcasting on the internet.

19. *Prepare your work meals in advance.* If you prepare food for lunch or breaks in advance, you will prevent meal preparation from taking away from valuable work time. It will also **39**

keep you from having to think about what you want to eat later too.

20. ***Over-communicate with colleagues and clients.*** This is a particular concern for those working remotely. Remind those who need to know frequently about your schedule, and tell them when you have finished a task. You don't have to write an essay about it, but let them know what's happening and repeat yourself as necessary. It's easy for clients and colleagues to forget you're there when you're not in an office together, so remind them by communicating frequently. Tell them again and again about any changes to your schedule, like if you are planning to take a vacation or need a break. Doing so will help ensure there are no problems when it comes time for change.

21. ***Take sick days.*** You will want to make your work-at-home situation as similar to any other job as possible. That means you should also take time off if you're sick. If you're making your own contracts, be sure and let clients know your policy about these situations. It is really better for everyone involved if you take the time you need to heal, since working while you're sick will affect the quality of your work and your productivity.

22. ***Show up to meetings and be heard.*** It's really easy for colleagues and superiors who are not working from home to forget that your opinions count too. So, when there's a meeting and even if it's not offered, ask to be included via video conferencing. Make sure you speak up and contribute to the meeting to let people know you're there. Even if that just means saying "Hello" to everyone when the meeting is starting, speaking up will make your presence known.

23. ***Use a secured virtual private network (VPN).*** Using a VPN is a security measure you can use to protect your privacy whenever you're connected to a network you don't control. This is

important if you're ever working not just from an internet cafe, library, or airport, but also when you're accessing certain servers or websites. In case of the latter, it can help you access the information you may not otherwise be able to get. Since you are now the one who must take care of any IT problems, you'll want to make sure your computer and internet network are safe. Using a VPN whenever you need to log in with a password is a great indicator for knowing when to do that.

Once again, this is not an exhaustive list of tips to help you prepare for working at home, but it's still a great start. Working from home takes a bit more self-discipline, but these tips should help make it easier. Once you get used to your office being in your home, you'll start treating that space just like you would any other office.

Now, imagine if all employee workspaces were like this. Your boss respects that you are working on a task and they recognize that they need to wait another 17 minutes until you are available. You don't have to worry about an angry call from a colleague who sent you an urgent email—today's 7th—half an hour ago, and you have not yet taken care of what they need. You can achieve these things at home. Following my guidelines can make working from home several times more productive as compared to working at the office.

The next question is where to find those work-from-home opportunities, which is something we'll tackle in subsequent chapters.

Chapter Summary

In this chapter, we've discussed some general forms of remote work that's available. Specifically, we've covered the following topics:

- Work from home options.
- The most popular jobs for remote workers.
- 23 tips for working from home.
- Treating your home office like any other office.

In the next chapter, we will be taking a look at the definition and distinction of freelance work from contractors and traditional employment. We'll also be examining the pros and cons of each.

[5] https://www.flexjobs.com/blog/post/20-most-common-work-from-home-job-titles-v2/

[6] https://www.inc.com/minda-zetlin/productivity-workday-52-minutes-work-17-minutes-break-travis-bradberry-pomodoro-technique.html

[7] Minds and brains of media multitaskers: Current findings and future directions. Proceedings of the National Academy of Sciences, 115(40), 9889–9896. https://doi.org/10.1073/pnas.1611612115

Chapter THREE

FREELANCE WORK

LET'S start with the definition of a freelance worker. Typically, this is someone who offers their services for a fee, but without the expectation of a permanent, single client. Now, you might have repeated clients or clients for whom you work on a regular basis, but usually, freelance work means working from one contract to another. It's a form of self-employment that is similar to operating your own home business. Let's take a closer look at the definition of a freelance worker versus contractors and regular employees:

1. *Freelancer*—this title means you're self-employed, pay your own taxes, don't usually have your own employees, have full control over where you work, likely have several clients and projects, determine your own rates, and usually work on smaller, shorter-term projects with clients. However, with being a freelancer, you would not be receiving company benefits.

2. *Contractor*—this can apply to freelance work, as some freelancers are contractors, but it's important to note the few

distinctions between typical freelance work and that of contractors. As a contractor—like a freelancer—you generally set your own work hours, have full control over the work you take on, and you can advertise your services for new business. Also like freelancers, you are self-employed and responsible for handling your own benefits and taxes. Some contractors work through an agency—in that case, they are more similar to a regular employee.

The main difference between contractors and freelancers in how contractors tend to work on one large project with a single client at a time. Also, while contract work can happen remotely, it happens more frequently on a client's worksite or in their offices.

These two forms of self-employment differ from a regular employee in the following four ways:

- An employee typically works for one company permanently and gets paid regularly, whether that be hourly, salaried, on a commission, or a combination of those forms of pay.

- Most employees work from a company office; although, some do negotiate remote work from home on certain days.

- Most employees work within the confines of a contract or job description that details their salary and work hours. The company typically determines when and where the employee will work.

- Most employees rely on their employer to withhold the proper taxes, which are usually deducted from their wages automatically.

According to an independent study by Upwork and Freelancers Union, the majority of American workers will be full or part-time freelancers by the year 2027[8] (2017). The situation with the coronavirus may have accelerated that projection, giving you the opportunity to get in ahead of the trend. But why is freelance work so popular?

Freelance Popularity

From a corporate perspective, freelancers and contract workers give the company more agility, as these workers can respond to its needs at any given time. Full-time employees cost thousands in benefits and other expenses, even when work is slow, so hiring freelancers offers a solution to that problem. Furthermore, hiring freelance workers means the employer doesn't have to pay for idle time, such as vacations, sick leave, training, and business travel. Also, remember that the best employees are usually already working, which means the employer is left with deciding between hiring an average employee who may not be up to the challenging tasks, or hiring a star and having to overpay that person later. With freelancing, an employer can hire the perfect employee for the job description. In that way, freelancers provide added value for their clients.

Freelancing does offer the workers certain advantages, though it's important to consider the drawbacks and prepare for those as well. One of the best things about freelance work is flexible hours, which allows for a healthier balance between work and personal life. While there exists the possibility that you'll experience long periods of no work, most freelancers choose this lifestyle because they want it and find it a better fit for their current goals and needs—not because it's the last resort. Still, there are some important things to consider before deciding to freelance.

□ **Insurance**

If you're working for an employer, they will typically have an insurance plan to offer you as a benefit, but as a freelancer, you will have to find your own insurance plan. You'll also want to provide for a retirement fund. These costs need to be part of the consideration when you bill clients. You need to break up the total cost into a per-project fee that covers your expenses.

Still, most freelancers find that they take home more money, even though they have to pay for their own benefits.

Freelance success mean marketing

Since you'll be on your own as a freelancer, you will need to prepare to market yourself and your work. You bear the burden of finding new clients and selling your talents to them, which often means a lot of unpaid work associated with prospecting, networking, winning a job offer, accounting, and various other administrative tasks. These are all unbillable hours, but they are critical for success.

The good news is that, as you do more great work, you won't have to work as hard to market yourself. You'll develop a portfolio that will do some of the work for you. Also, word-of-mouth advertising can bring clients to your business without you having to seek them out. Once you are approached by a client, you can usually charge more than if you had to seek them out manually.

Flexible hours

Perhaps the biggest draw of freelance work, as mentioned, is the freedom to set your own hours. Though you might be working more than 40 hours per week, you can arrange those hours to suit your schedule better. One of the drawbacks to that, however, is that there is no such thing as a paid vacation. If you take time off for any reason, that means you're not making money for that amount of time. Still, with good planning, you'll find you can enjoy all the benefits of a flexible work schedule, including taking vacations without having to worry about lost wages. The most important thing to ensure is that you keep good communication with your valued clients, so they can know your availability.

47

▫ **Physical limitations**

For those with physical limitations, freelance work can give them the flexibility they need. In fact, 46% of freelancers are unable to work in a traditional job because of physically limiting personal circumstances[9] (Upwork, 2019).

▫ **Quick start up**

Starting out as a freelancer is affordable, quick, and relatively easy, especially when compared to other forms of self-employment. In addition, as soon as you can find a client, you can then start getting paid, which may be even faster than getting employed.

▫ **You name your price**

Freelancing doesn't come with a set salary and, of course, the work is not necessarily consistent. For this reason, you have to consider your extraneous costs carefully, which would normally fall to the employer in a traditional job. You have to keep careful track of those expenses, so you can build those costs into your estimates.

One good way to establish your freelance fees is to know exactly what the costs of running your business are and make a list for them, so you can then add a percentage to the fee for each project. You'll want to consider your standard bills like electricity, internet/phone connection, mortgage/rent, office costs including equipment (computers, software, maintenance) office supplies (paper, ink, pens, and paper clips), and any other services you pay for like domain costs, invoicing platforms, media spending, and the various add-ons related to your profession.

Once you have a list of your costs per month, you can calculate your freelance rate baseline. You can then add on a safety cushion and percentage for your profit. Another way to do it is to take your yearly gross income for a similar job, add 25% to 45% for your insurance and admin costs, the safety cushion, and profit. Then, divide that by 250 working days. Finally, divide that number by 8 hours per day working, and you will then have an estimate of an hourly fee. We'll cover this more in detail in subsequent chapters, but suffice it to say that you will have to figure out how much you want to charge clients for your services, and you will have to take these into consideration to ensure you're making enough money to live and thrive.

Comparisons— Traditional Employment versus Freelance Work

It might also help—when trying to decide on whether to become a freelancer—to look at some of the pros and cons of freelance work compared to traditional employee work. The money and lifestyle can be radically different between the two. So, is freelance work right for you, or should you stick with more traditional types of employment? The following sections will go over some considerations to consider when deciding between the two.

Steady income and benefits—this is one of the biggest arguments in favor of traditional employment. Most companies offer health insurance along with some kind of retirement planning. There is also the subject about paid vacations. Freelancers, on the other hand, do have to pay for their own benefits and won't have the benefit of paid vacations. Also, while regular employees know the wage they will be earning, freelance income can fluctuate dramatically—one month, you might be working on a couple big projects and earning double compared to the traditional employee; however, in the next month, you might only have one job that pays just a few hundred dollars upon completion.

Income potential—Freelancers have the most income potential. If you're working a traditional job, you may have opportunities for growth, but those are determined by your employer, typically with an upper limit. If you're a freelancer, you would be determining your growth opportunities, setting your own rates, and won't have any limits on your income. As long as you are good at finding clients, marketing yourself, and can complete your projects, the sky will literally be the limit for you. There are many freelancers that do their jobs so excellently that they have a full agenda with clients competing for them. As a freelancer, being great at one high-value skill can be a great asset when picking up clients.

Taxes—taxes are the needles in everyone's sides. With traditional employment, taxes are deducted from your paycheck and filing each year is usually a much simpler process. However, as a free-lancer, you will be deducting business expenses, which can amount to significant savings. There are a number of things you can write off on your taxes, including a portion of your mortgage if you have a home office, the portion of your utilities that run your office, other home-related expenses, your office supplies, and any other business-related expenses. Those costs can really add up, which is why being a freelancer can be a great advantage.

Moreover, if you handle your freelance business right, you'll also be able to avoid high self-employment taxes (we'll discuss this in a later chapter). If your entire income for any given year comes from freelance work, you'll likely have to pay something in taxes, as opposed to traditional employment where most employees would receive a tax refund. So, if you choose freelance work, you will need to plan for that.

Growth opportunities—as a traditional employee, you would usually have the opportunity to climb the corporate ladder. This can allow you to increase your income and status significantly. However, such will often involve a trade-off that will impact the amount of quality time you would get to spend with your family.

Still, the path for professional growth is usually laid out clearly with traditional employment.

On the other hand, as a freelancer, you're starting out at the top of your ladder. Freelancers have more work opportunities. There is a wider variety of project possibilities to choose from, which provides the freelancer with a level of freedom that the traditional employee simply doesn't have. As an employee, you might have proven you are well-qualified and experienced for a promotion, but as long as the position is occupied, you will likely get nowhere. You may get a promise one year, but then the next year, you may get an excuse for why you were not promoted... again. In this case, you are limited only to those job positions within your company and for which you have the appropriate skills. As a freelancer, those limits don't apply, and you can give yourself a promotion at any time!

Social interactions—Traditional employees have one thing that freelancers don't: a regular group of people they see in person and with whom they can socialize. This can lead to some fulfilling work experiences and can amount to an important part of your social life. On the other hand, freelancers have more lifestyle flexibility and don't have to deal with any office politics or drama it creates. Furthermore, freelancers get to choose when and where they work, giving them the freedom to adjust their schedules around the requirements of their social lives. If you have children, freelancing can have some great flexibility benefits for you.

Even the most flexible employers can't compare to the freedom of freelance work. However, you should note before deciding on freelancing for this perk alone that this freedom can easily turn into loneliness. Freelancers have to find socializing options, like having shared offices with others or even joining a freelance professional organization or club if they want to stay healthy within the profession. Finding more people in the same niche gives you the opportunity to talk about the challenges of your work. 51

Job security—while there is more income security with traditional jobs, the security of the job itself isn't always assured. Because the traditional employee only has one "client," they are more at risk than most freelancers who work with several clients. Even if you work in a large company, recent events such as the Great Recession of 2008 and the current Coronavirus crisis have demonstrated that traditional work may not offer as much security as one would hope. On the other hand, freelancers have multiple clients, and if they lose one, they would likely still have others to work with while they look for more. Yes, they may have to stay on their toes and fight harder for those clients, but they also learn quickly how to secure new clients and keep them. That can be better than what is often a false sense of security you would get with traditional employment.

Self-discipline—while traditional employment requires a basic level of self-discipline (getting up, getting to work on time, doing what you're expected to do, etc.), freelance work takes that requirement to a whole new level. Freelancers have to be self-starters and always looking for the next job.

As a freelancer, you have to become comfortable with marketing yourself, winning over clients, drumming up your business, and making sure you get paid. You're much more likely to get rejected as a freelancer than with traditional employment, and that uncertainty can definitely become a source of stress.

So, what is right for you? In these uncertain times, we've definitely seen the drawbacks of relying on traditional forms of employment. However, if your company is amenable to the idea, it might be a good compromise for you if your job allows you to work from home. This is not a solution, however, for employees for whom telecommuting or working at home is not an option, such as wait staff and other service industry employees. For those individuals,

it might certainly be worth taking a chance as a freelancer.

The best thing you can do to decide is to be honest with yourself about your personality—are you self-disciplined and self-motivated? Are you attentive to details? Do you value flexibility over steady employment? If you can answer yes to these questions, then freelance work might be just the right fit. The following list contains a few more points to consider as you make your decision:

- Freelancer work can be more enjoyable because it provides only value to the client. On the other hand, employees spend a significant portion of their time reviewing company emails and attending meetings that may not be directly relevant to their work.

- It is often difficult to get a good job as an employee. Interview questions may include why were you terminated from a previous job or why you left, which can be difficult to answer. Freelancers are simply hired based on their portfolio of previous work.

- Salaries are fixed expenses that increase when a new employee is hired. Freelancers offer great flexibility to clients and can agree on an hourly fee, and more work (expenses) is related to revenue increases, meaning that hiring freelancers is always profitable.

- As an employee, you can be overeducated for the job and underpaid.

- During crises, employers reduce both staff and salaries. If the employee has any option, it is to choose between staying with a lower salary or searching for another employer, neither of which is optimal.

- When the client's business declines, the freelancer can already be contracting for more work from other clients.

- It is more costly to live as an employee because of various factors like commuting expenses or buying lunch every day.

- Many managers are position leaders, and it can often be stressful and discouraging to work in those conditions. As a freelancer, you would only have to deal with the product/service you are delivering, and you wouldn't have to account for the actions of others.

This chapter should have given you some good information to consider in terms of the benefits that can come with freelance work. Informed decisions usually produce the best results!

Chapter Summary

In this chapter, we discussed freelance work definitions, along with its pros and cons. Specifically, we've covered the following topics:

- Freelancer definition.
- Contractor definition.
- Traditional employee definition.
- Growing freelance popularity.
- Freelance work benefits.
- Freelance work as compared to traditional employment.

In the next chapter, we will be talking about what it takes to get set up as a freelancer.

[8] https://www.upwork.com/press/2017/10/17/freelancing-in-america-2017/
[9] https://www.upwork.com/i/freelancing-in-america/

Chapter **FOUR**

HOW TO GET SET UP AS FREELANCER

SETTING up freelance work can be really easy to do—it takes less than a day and requires little to no cash upfront. You can start working as a freelancer simply and without creating a business entity, but there are some important considerations if you choose that path. First of all, if you don't create a business entity, you will, by default, be considered a sole proprietorship with unlimited liability. The most significant consideration with this fact is that, if you're sued, your personal assets will be at risk.

Additionally, without a business entity, you will face much higher self-employment taxes. Therefore, it's highly recommended that you create a **limited liability company** (LLC). Doing so shields your personal assets from a lawsuit, and in the event you lose and cannot pay, the company can be dissolved. However, before we get too deep into that, let's just start at the beginning. You've decided, like more than 56 million US citizens[10] (Stolzoff, 2018), that freelancing is right for you. How do you begin?

Step #1: Define Your Goals

The first thing you want to do is to define your measurable goals clearly. Without that, you'll find yourself faltering at the outset. You don't want just to set your ultimate goal; you need to describe the steps it will take to get there clearly. Begin by answering the following questions:

- Is freelancing going to be your primary source of income or just a side job; or, will it just be a way to get through the current crisis?

- Are you using freelancing as a stepping stone to some other goal?

- Do you want to do freelance work because of the lifestyle benefits associated with being your own boss?

Regardless of your goals, make them abundantly clear. For example, your goal might be to be fully self-employed through freelancing. Otherwise, your goal could be associated more with doing something you truly love. Whatever your goals are, write them down in as much detail as you can. Don't just say, "My goal is to get rich;" instead say, "My goal is to make a minimum of $100,000 per year with freelance work."

Please remember that goals should be specific with regard to what you want to do, how much you want to wear, and when you want to achieve that level of income. You may be wondering about the possibility of your goals changing. You are right—they not only might change, but it's also almost certain they will. That's okay because, as you move through the process, you'll find alternatives that will suit you better. However, if you start with vague goals, those will likely lead nowhere and you'll have difficulty measuring any progress you're making.

Along these same lines, you will want to decide on the exact kind of freelance work you will be doing. Will you be writing, designing, **57** or developing something? What kind of work will you be doing? Once you have clarity around that, you can then begin to outline shorter-term goals and benchmarks that will help get you closer to your ultimate goals.

Let's look at an example—you have a goal to be fully self-employed as a freelance worker because you want to set your own hours, decide who to work with, and call your own shots. The next question is: how do you get there? One of the first steps, regardless of the type of freelance work you want to do, is to get your income up to a sustainable level prior to quitting your day job. During this coronavirus crisis, you may not have the luxury of doing that, but if you do, it's advisable to wait to quit your job until your freelance income is at least 75% of what your job is paying you.

Without that luxury, you'll have to dive right into freelance work to start earning a paycheck as quickly as possible. You can do that, but you would still need to lay out your income target for freelance work, along with some realistic expectations in terms of how much time you will have to devote to your freelance jobs and the income they will bring you. To calculate your needs, add up all of your living expenses, including the things you want to be able to do, but can't do currently based on your present income. Then, add a security cushion and a profit margin, which should give you a rough idea of the income you need to sustain yourself. Once you do all that, you're finally ready for the next step.

Additionally, you should remember that a great advantage of being a freelancer is saving on expenses. You're staying at home and saving on travel expenses, along with other kinds of expenses such as restaurants. This amounts to hundreds of dollars every month.

If you would like to learn more about personal finances for free-lancers, check out the other book I wrote, *Save Money and Spend Wisely During and After the Economic Crisis*. You will learn even more practical tips to start saving hundreds a month from today.

Step #2: Research the Industry

You want to do a little market research in the area of free-lancing in which you're hoping to work. Who are your customers and competitors? What can you offer your clients that the competition can't? Is there something different that you do in that niche that your clients will appreciate? Try to find how you are different from the majority. Are you faster, lower in cost, or unique in anything you provide?

Also, do a little research into what your competitors are charging. You don't want to try to charge less than all of your competitors, but you want to price yourself somewhere in the middle. The point you'll make to the client is that you offer quality services that are worth the price, even if that price is higher than other freelancers offering the same thing. You can always list your services on freelance work sites, but you will likely be paid less than what you're worth. However, to start earning some money and getting your name out there, freelance work sites are great options that will be described later in the book.

Researching the industry is also important for finding a profitable niche. By doing that, you'll be competing on value rather than price. For example, rather than simply taking any and all graphic design projects, concentrating on one profitable niche, such as infographic design for startup blogs, will help you deliver real quality for your clients better, and your clients will appreciate—and pay for—those kinds of services. Doing so will also allow you to choose a niche that truly interests you, which will serve to keep you motivated as well. Along with that, while most successful freelancers start with just one specific service, if you are great at other related fields, you can also offer those services to your satisfied customers.

Step #3: Establish Your Business Entity

As we've mentioned, you can work as a freelancer without a business entity, but such is really not advisable, particularly if you plan to make this venture a permanent change. There are four ways you can structure your business entity:

- Sole proprietorship

- Partnership

- Limited Liability Company (LLC)

- Corporation

Most freelancers opt for a sole proprietorship as, as previously discussed, this is the default if you don't register with the state. However, as also discussed, the problem with this option is that, with a sole proprietorship and a partnership, your personal assets are at risk if you are sued. That's because, with these entities, there's no separation between you and the business, which is all why an LLC, S-Corp, or C-Corp might be the better choices. With these entities, you are the owner of the business and, if someone wants to sue, they would be suing the business rather than you.

LLC and corporations offer limited liability, so if you are sued, your personal and family assets would stay safe. An important difference between the forms, however, is that they are taxed differently. C-Corps must pay corporate taxes, whereas LLCs and S-Corps are what are called *pass-through or tax disregarded entities.* Their profits are passed through to the owner, who can then report gains and/or losses on their personal tax returns.

With C-Corps, the corporation pays taxes, and any dividends paid to shareholders—which would include you as the owner— would be taxed as well. Because of this "double taxation" potential, many business owners prefer to go with an S-Corps or LLC. However, new laws have reduced the tax burden on C-Corps, and that fact, along with the other benefits of C-Corps—such as insurance options—might make it the better option. Before creating your business entity, you might want to take the time to consult with an accountant to see what will work best for you.

Step #4: Identify Your Clients

To really be effective as a freelancer, you will have to identify your target clients. When you're first starting out, you might take any clients who will hire you, but you would really want to think about who will benefit the most from your services. Who are the right clients for your freelance work? Thinking about this consideration will help you to target your marketing better to those who are most likely to need you. Also, once you've landed a few clients in your focused niche, it's likely the word will get around to other potential clients about your services, which can bring clients to you instead of you having to go search them yourself.

Focusing in on specific clients can be a difficult decision to make because you might have to turn away much needed business; however, once you narrow down your target clients, you will have better success in the long run. If you begin with a few clients who really like your work, that momentum can pick up quickly. Focusing on your target clients also allows you to produce higher quality work and compete on value rather than price. Happy clients then become your sales force, which can help you become the go-to resource in your niche. It will also allow you to charge clients premium rates for your services.

To determine your ideal client, ask yourself the following questions:

- Who will find my services useful?

- Will my clients be larger corporations, smaller businesses, or individual clients?

- Where are they located?

- Why will they find my services valuable?

- Who can afford to pay what I charge?

- Who, within the business, makes the decisions about hiring freelance work?

- Can I find a way to connect with them on a personal level?

Be specific in answering these questions, so you can define your typical client. Once you have this information, you can create a cold email (unsolicited email) that cuts to the core needs of your ideal clients, helps you connect with them, and allows you to offer them an immediate value. If you try to be everything to everybody, you will get nothing. If, on the other hand, you choose a very narrow niche of customers, you can make a quick breakthrough and become very attractive to that small group of clients.

If you have a favorite restaurant, why is that? Usually, it's because they have something that suits you well. It can be a specific food, waiter, the space, music, or the other guests you meet there. As long as the restaurant continues with what you like, you will be their regular customer. Even if the restaurant does not have a lot of other customers, it can still be successful with a small and select group of satisfied customers. That is exactly what you want to do—build a select group of satisfied clients who will use your services regularly.

If you're not sure how to identify your ideal client, study your network of prior employers, previous clients, or even suppliers for your previous boss. You could also observe a good colleague or friend who epitomizes your perfect client. Think about it this way—if you were telling your best friend about your services, which friend would you choose, and what benefits would you tell them about in terms of what you're offering?

Step #5: Set Strategic Prices

There are a number of helpful websites out there that can assist you when trying to decide how much you want to charge. The first thing to remember is that you are not pricing your services based on what your competitors are charging; rather, you want to charge your services based on the quality and value you provide your clients. Part of setting your prices will depend on the type of clients you're targeting.

Really, there is no such thing as prices that are too high—they may be too high for the clients you're targeting, but there are some clients out there for whom they will not be too high. Therefore, you need to do your homework and find out the price range of the clients you want to target. Then, you can pitch your services to them at a price they can justify because of the quality and value of work you provide. One thing about pricing—many freelancers find that the more they charge, the less clients complain, and you can choose to offer your services to clients with bigger budgets.

The other thing to remember about pricing is that you need to make sure you charge enough to cover your living expenses, along with a decent profit. Here's one way you can calculate an hourly rate:

- Begin with your target annual salary—for example, $75,000 per year.

- Factor in your new expenses and overhead as a self-employed freelancer—let's say, another $22,513. That would mean that your new adjusted annual income will be $97,513.

- Determine your billable hours per year—the number of working hours per year is 2,080, but you would probably want to do freelance work to have a more flexible schedule and more time off. So, with three weeks of vacation, 7 US annual holidays, and 5 sick days, that would come to 216 hours fewer, or 1,864 hours.

But, that's not all—you have to account for the non-billable hours that you would be spending searching for new clients, responding to emails, and other administrative types of work. A good rule of thumb is to allow for 25% of your hours to be spent on non-billable activities. That would mean 1,864 multiplied by .75, which equals 1,398 billable hours per year.

- Last, divide the adjusted annual salary (in this example, $97,513) by the adjusted billable hours per year of 1,398. That would come down to $69.75 per hour, and it's okay to round that up to $70 per hour.

Once you have an hourly rate, you can determine what you would charge for salaried work or by contract much more easily. You need to be ready with different pricing models for various projects or clients. The pros of the hourly rate are that clients are familiar with the concept, and it is the most common pricing model for freelance work. Also, it's easy to keep track of your hours using various time-tracking programs that are already readily available. Moreover, hourly rates are easy to negotiate. You know the hourly rate you need to charge for your desired annual income, and from there, you can pre-define an expedited services rate quite easily. Lastly, pricing per hour gives you more flexibility with the client, particularly if they continue to try adding extra services they want you to complete. It's much easier to adjust and negotiate pricing in this scenario if you're using an hourly rate model because they would be paying for that extra time.

The drawbacks of the hourly model stem from how clients will often want to know the total price of a project. Even a few hundred dollars difference in costs can make a huge difference for small business clients. Also, if you put your hourly rate on your website, it will give you less negotiating power for more complex or demanding projects. Finally, you will be penalized by hourly rates if you're fast, and delivering high-quality services quickly should be a well-paid attribute rather than a penalty.

Another type of pricing model is known as a monthly retainer, which is usually used by more experienced and established free-lancers. With this model, the client would pay you on a recurring basis and in advance. You get a fixed amount each month, regardless of whether you worked for the client that particular month. Essentially, they're paying to have you there when they need your services. This can be good for both sides, but it can also go bad quickly. To use this model, you need to have a clear agreement on what projects are included in your retainer price, and what services might incur additional fees. This information would be stated plainly in a contract that both parties would sign.

The benefits of a monthly retainer are that you would receive steady pay, which can help both you and your client feel safe in the contract. The client gets a significant advantage as well, since they have you on retainer, so you're available for the agreed-upon work. They also don't have to pay overhead costs as they would for an employee. However, the drawbacks include how the client will think of your services as on-demand, and they'll expect an immediate response from you whenever they need. That can feel a lot like a boss. Also, just as your client comes to be dependent on you, you may come to depend on their monthly check, which can be a problem if you lose that client for any reason. Thus, even in this situation, you would still have to prioritize getting more clients, and doing so can be difficult because you would have less time for other clients.

Another model would be a contract-by-contract basis for your freelance work. That can give a steady income over the course of the contract, but there are a lot of considerations for how to design that contract. For example, for particularly long-term projects, you'll want to get paid for meeting certain milestones so you won't have to wait until the contract has ended to get paid. Of course, for setting the entire price of the contract, you will have to estimate your hours in advance, which can be tricky if you don't have a good grasp on how long it will take you to do the job.

One way to get around this problem is to set an hourly rate as part of the contract, along with an estimated time to complete the work. Once you do that, you can then include a clause that states, in essence, that work that goes above and beyond the estimate will incur additional labor costs. That gives you some leeway; however, you would really need to make sure you do a good job of estimating the time it will take you to do the work. Enacting that "additional costs" clause should be the exception, not the rule.

Another good pricing strategy is to set a low price for the basic product, then you can add extra costs for additional work. For example, a designer can charge for one proposal with one revision, then offer more designs and revisions for an extra cost. This pricing would likely appear fair to clients because they know what they are paying for and can choose different packages. The benefits of this model for the client include how they would gain a better estimate for the total cost of the project.

It's also important to understand that there are certain types of jobs in which specific pricing models would work. For example, no client would pay a designer or a web developer hourly because they cannot control how intensively the freelancer is working. On the other hand, jobs like a virtual assistant, medical assistant, or telephonist would normally be paid based on time. Before you set your pricing strategy, it's helpful to research what pricing methods are used most often in your field of choice.

In the end, if you start out using one pricing model, then find it isn't helping you reach your desired income, there are alternatives. You can change the model you use or vary your model based on the client. You're not necessarily locked into one model—just be sure to indicate that there are different pricing models depending on the client needs indicated on your website and in your promotional materials and offers.

Step #6: Set Up a Website

Now that you have identified your ideal client and established your pricing model(s), it's time to set up a website with that client in mind, so you can communicate the services you're offering effectively. With your business entity established—or at least, your business name—it's a good idea to go ahead and buy a domain name for your website. They are often fairly and reasonably priced (usually starting from $1 per month), and they help clients remember where they can go to find you. You'll want to think carefully in terms of naming the website, and you can incorporate your business name with your specialty, such as BostonBlogWriter.com.

Once you have a domain name, you can set up a high-quality website. One thing you can try with your website is create a portfolio containing services you offer. Remember—this is the first impression that many potential clients will have of you, so you need to show good communication, display exactly what your services are for, who they are for, and why you are the best person for the job. Be short and to the point because people do not read websites; they scroll through them with eyes and notice visuals, bold words, and only the information they need. To be effective, your freelance portfolio website will need to contain the following items:

- A description of your services and specialties, along with specific examples of your work.

- Your contact information.

- An email subscriber link.

- Your relevant skills, education, and accomplishments.

- Client testimonials—if you don't have any, you can ask former or current coworkers or bosses to provide testimonials of your work.

- Regular updates that show your evolution, new clients, and updates of your sample work.

In addition to these items, you also want your website to show off a bit of your personality. Be professional albeit true to yourself. Check out other freelance websites to get some ideas and inspiration on how to position yourself in your niche. If you can afford to do so, it might also be worth your while to hire a web designer. There are a number of freelance pages where you can find great freelancers for web page development for some low prices. Your website is not something to skimp on, so getting a professional web designer can really help make your website look and feel official. There is a certain psychology behind building a website in a way that will make others trust it and you, and it's important to understand that while designing your website[11] (Kachan, 2019).

Step #7: Take Care of Business

There are a couple things you'll want to do as a newly established, self-employed worker. First, you'll want to make sure you have all the required business licenses pertaining to your profession. In some locations, even freelancers are required to have business licenses. You don't want to get caught having to pay a penalty because you didn't have the proper city, county, or state licenses, so check those out for your area and make sure you're in compliance.

Next, it might serve you well to get an Employer Identification Number (EIN). An EIN is helpful for business documents and if you should find yourself needing to hire or outsource work for a project. It also helps keep your social security number from becoming vulnerable to theft.

Another thing you'll probably want to do is open a bank account for your business. It's really smart to keep your business and personal bank accounts separate, as doing so will help with accounting when tax time comes around, so that you can know how much you earned from your business better. Choose a bank that specializes in small businesses and offers good packages for reasonably low prices.

Step # 8: Set Up Profiles on Freelance Job Sites

This is one way to find freelance gigs. There are a number of freelance work sites, such as Upwork, Freelancer.com, among others where you can create a profile that caters to the clients you're looking to find. By creating a profile, you can both apply for jobs and receive offers from clients who have seen your profile. This may not be your main source of work, but it can get you started and give you some valuable experience. We will be discussing these freelance job sites more in the next chapter—just remember that this can be a good way to pick up side jobs after you've secured a few steady clients.

Step #9: Marketing

Even before officially launching your freelance business, you'll want to make sure you have laid the groundwork for marketing **69** your work. You want to create social media profiles everywhere you think your ideal clients spend time. It's also worthwhile to go ahead and write several blog posts so you can give that audience plenty of content to explore. Plus, it's helpful to have several blog posts in a queue and ready to publish so you can send out new messages inviting potential clients to read your latest blog posts. When clients read valuable posts, they will think, "This freelancer seems really knowledgeable about this topic, I want to hire them." Having them ready means that, once everything else is ready, you can just post and send out messages without having to do extra work.

You'll also want to link your messages and ads to examples of your work, along with your pricing structure and contact information. It's also helpful to go ahead and get familiar with an email marketing software, so you can use it once you have an email subscriber list. If you feel comfortable doing so, you can also reach out to your personal network to market your start in this new freelance career. Let others know you would appreciate any business referrals they might provide. As part of a marketing strategy, it might also be helpful to brainstorm with other freelancers or even partner with them to get more business. You can also barter your services for theirs.

Step #10: Plan Your Launch

You want to start out with a bang, so to speak, by creating buzz around the launch of your new freelancing career. You can start a Facebook Live video, create flyers, use a direct mail campaign, or offer some promotions on your opening day, for example. You can also offer discounts or something like, "Two free blog posts if you buy 10!" if one of your main gigs is writing blog posts. Do what you can to get people interested in what you're offering and create some incentives that can help push them in your direction. Once you've hooked some clients in, you have to deliver on the goods. It's also good to offer occasional promotions even after your launch, which can help generate new clients while maintaining those whom you have already established.

Chapter Summary

In this chapter, we discussed how to get started as a freelancer worker. Specifically, we went over the following topics:

- Defining your specific goals.
- Finding your niche.
- Establishing your business entity.
- Identifying your clients.
- Setting strategic prices.
- Different price models.
- Setting up a website.
- Taking care of business by getting any required licenses, opening a bank account, and getting an EIN number.
- Setting up profiles on freelance job sites.
- Marketing.
- Planning your launch.

In the next chapter, we will be discussing remote work examples and various sites you can use for remote work.

---

[10] https://qz.com/work/1441108/the-us-now-has-more-than-56-7-million-freelance-workers-and-they-vote/

[11] https://www.business2community.com/web-design/psychology-in-web-design-exploring-hidden-influences-on-users-decision-making-02200931

Chapter FIVE

REMOTE WORK EXAMPLES AND SITES

NOW that you've decided to become a freelance worker, it's helpful to discuss some specifics about freelance work and job sites. One of the most common questions is about where to find good paying freelance work.

Finding Well-Paying Freelance Work

Many freelancers can earn $90,000 per year or more. In fact, among the more than 15 million full-time freelance workers, over 3 million are earning over $100,000 per year[12] (Braverman Rega, 2019). There is also an increasing demand for highly skilled freelance workers. With nearly 60 million Americans engaging in either full-time or part-time freelance work, the market is now getting quite competitive. Still, if you're looking to make good money, you might want to consider the following highest paying job categories for freelance work, identified by Upwork (Braverman Rega, 2019):

Income of $150,000+ per year

◻ *Corporate law*—examples in this category include intellectual property attorneys and corporate legal counsel. Individuals working freelance in corporate law make an average of $85 per hour with a potential annual income of $170,000 or more.

◻ *Contract law*—positions within this niche include litigators, general counsel, and attorneys who draft contracts. These freelance workers earn an average of $75 per hour with a potential income of $150,000 per year.

Income of $100,000 to $150,000 per year

◻ *Financial planner*—examples in this category include experts in financial modeling, CPAs, and financial estate-planning attorneys. These individuals make an average of $62.50 per hour and have a potential annual income of $125,000 per year.

◻ *Management consulting*—this category includes business consultants, and they make an average of $60 per hour with a potential annual income of $120,000 per year.

◻ *ERP/CRM software*—solution architects, consultants, and software developers are examples in this category. These individuals also make approximately $60 per hour and can make up to $120,000 per year.

◻ *Network and system administration*—network architects and IT administrators can make up to $120,000 per year with an average hourly wage of $60.

◻ *Data visualization*—examples in this category include developers, programmers, data visualization analysts, and survey and research design consultants. These individuals make approximately $50 per hour and can earn as much as $100,000 per year.

- *Machine learning*—deep learning analytics consultants and predictive analytics consultants are examples in this category. These individuals also make around $100,000 per year and have an average hourly wage of $50.

- *Quantitative analysis*—professors of economics and statistical analysts are two examples within this category. These individuals make an average hourly wage of $50 with an annual earning potential of $100,000.

- *Presentations*—examples here include presentation designers and writers, and this is another category where the average hourly wage is $50 and the annual earning potential is $100,000.

- *Database administration*—examples here include data engineers and systems engineers, also with an average hourly wage of $50 and an annual earning potential of $100,000.

- *Display advertising*—examples in this category include graphic designers and internet marketers. The hourly wage is $50 and the potential annual rate is $100,000.

- *Email and marketing automation*—examples for this category include marketing experts, developers, senior marketing strategists, and consultants. The hourly rate is typically $50 per hour and the annual earning potential is $100,000.

- *Marketing strategy*—titles in this category include digital marketing consultants, copywriters, and B2B marketing specialists. The average hourly rate is $50 per hour with an annual earning potential of $100,000.

- *Search Engine Marketing (SEM)*—one example in this category is Google AdWord experts, and it also has an average hourly rate of $50 per hour with a potential annual rate of $100,000.

- *Desktop software development*—sample titles in this category include full-stack senior web developers and customer software developers. This niche has an average hourly rate of $50 per hour with an annual earning potential of $100,000.

- *E-commerce development*—examples in this category include developers, online marketing and e-commerce solutions experts, and e-commerce integration and automation consultants. This category also has an average hourly rate of $50 per hour with an annual earning potential of $100,000.

- *Mobile developer*—sample careers in this category include iOS developers, Android developers, and mobile app developers. This category has an average hourly rate of $50 per hour and an annual earning potential of $100,000.

Income of $90,000 to $100,000 per year

- *Scripts and Utilities*—the examples of careers in this category include Google Sheets experts, apps scripts experts, and Excel automation specialists. This category has an average hourly rate of $49 per hour with an annual earning potential of $98,000.

- *Physical design*—sample careers in this category include industrial design engineers, product developers, and global visual merchandising managers. This job category has an average hourly rate of $45 per hour with an annual earning potential of $90,000.

- *Mechanical engineering*—titles in this category include mechanical engineers, structural engineers, and designers. The average hourly rate for this category is $45 per hour with an annual earning potential of $90,000.

- *Product design*—sample careers in this category include user-experience consultants and product designers. The average hourly rate is $45 per hour with an annual earning potential of $90,000.

- *Web and mobile design*—careers in this category include web and mobile app developers and user-experience designers. The category has an average hourly rate of $45 and an annual earning potential of $90,000.

- *Web development*—sample careers in this category include full-stack web development, business systems experts, user-experience designers, and front-end developers. The hourly rate average is $45 per hour and the annual potential is $90,000.

- *Resumes and cover letters*—titles in this category include professional development writers, career coaches, and cover letter and LinkedIn support. The category has an average hourly rate of $45 per hour with an annual earning potential of $90,000.

These job categories were pulled from categories with more than 1,000 completed jobs between January 1, 2018 and December 1, 2019 (Braverman Rega, 2019). As you can see, none of the categories here have an annual income under $90,000, and these jobs have a variety of experience and educational requirements. Within some categories, experience alone could easily land you the job, whereas others may require more advanced education.

Regardless of the requirements, these job categories and their income potentials demonstrate that a successful and lucrative freelance career is not only possible, but becoming increasingly more common. While these categories represent the top earners, there are many more freelance jobs with an average income range that allows for comfortable living. But what about the freelance sites where you can find work? Let's look at a few of the better websites that help pair freelancers with employers.

Freelance Websites

Freelance websites are platforms that pair clients with freelancers.
It's a handy way to get started in the gig economy, and it can help

you grow your portfolio while you are first setting up your website online. You should still do whatever it is you need to do to get your freelancing career on track (getting appropriately educated, investing in the equipment you need, getting your branding in place). Once you do, you can then start working immediately by using these websites.

A great advantage of freelance websites is that they set rules about which freelancers and clients they will accept, reducing the time and costs associated with agreeing to specific conditions with your clients. The websites often check clients and freelancers to remove any scammers. They secure payment of fees usually in a way where the client pays the website; then, after confirming the product was delivered at the agreed quality level, the amount is released to the freelancer. This payment is often much faster than if the freelancer were in direct contact with the client. In case of disagreement, the website may act as a negotiator. Some websites charge fees to one or both parties; however, these fees are often well worth the benefits provided by the website.

Next, let's look at some of the better websites for finding freelance work!

General Freelance Work

These websites have a broad sampling of freelance jobs, regardless of your specialty area. There are jobs listed for virtually any kind of service you can provide.

▫ **FlexJobs.com**

This is a well-curated site that includes freelance and remote jobs. It also includes other types of gig work. The curators research the jobs and monitor new gigs thoroughly, so you don't have to worry about scam postings. However, regular access to jobs on this site is not free. Still, it might be worth the investment for your niche and, if you start earning immediately, it can pay for itself.

- **SolidGigs.com**

  This is a great site for finding freelance jobs fast. The SolidGigs team combs through numerous freelance job boards, and they send you the best 2% of jobs every week. Screening these jobs helps you because, otherwise, you would be doing that work. Therefore, the hours you would spend looking for the right job opportunities could then be spent pitching yourself or working. This site also has an enormous resource library you can take advantage of, including courses, interviews, templates, scripts, and other tools that can help you land more freelance work. Similar to the last, this site is not free, but it's a good investment to get both weekly gigs tailored to your niche and training resources.

- **Fiverr.com**

  This site takes its name from its design—every job starts at $5. That may sound low, but you can set up tiers that go above that base $5 option, and it all can add up fast. This site is a great way to get started immediately and build your portfolio. You will find this site attractive if you plan to offer standard products and services, such as a book cover design. Many small clients prefer this site because they can search the product or service category, compare freelancers' portfolios and prices, and make the entire purchase within a few minutes.

- **Upwork.com**

  Upwork was the combining result of two leading freelance job platforms—oDesk and Elance, and is now a huge job site. Upwork posts over 12 million freelancers, 5 million clients, and close to 3 million jobs each year. Thus, no matter your niche, you can find a job listed on this site. However, you have to consider that Upwork takes between a 5-20% cut from your earnings. You may also need to purchase points called connects that are required for applying for a job. One application costs between 30 and 90 cents, which is actually a good rule because it prevents certain freelancers from applying for every job. The jobs listed here are generally lower-priced; despite that, this is still the largest freelance platform in the world, and Fortune 500 businesses, along with other fast-growing startups, all use this platform to find freelancers.

Indeed.com

Indeed collects all kinds of job openings and puts them in one place. The site is easy to search through, with features to filter remote or on-site jobs. The best parts about this site are that it's free and you can place your resume on the site and apply quickly with a single click of a button.

Guru.com

This site makes it easy to create a profile that will show off your experience, which will make it easier for potential employers to contact you. There are also a massive amount of job postings every day, they allow you a decent amount of free applications, and they only charge a 9% commission.

TopTal.com

TopTal works exclusively with the best—top 3%—freelance software developers, designers, finance experts, product managers, and project managers in the world. They also work with the top companies looking to hire them. TopTal has a rigorous screening process; however, once you're in, you have a greater chance of landing high-paying jobs. Building a career on TopTal will skyrocket your experience because you will be working on the most important projects from leading companies.

Writer Freelance Websites

If you're a writer, these sites will help you find jobs specific to your niche. They will help you find the clients so you can spend more time working on your craft.

- **Contena.co**

  Contena provides a huge volume of well-paid jobs for writers, editors, and content creators of almost any kind. This site features a mix of freelance and full-time remote jobs, including relatively high paying jobs. One recent example was a $10,000 per month gig writing technical ebooks. The site boasts literally thousands of other opportunities across many industries involving trustworthy companies.

- **FreelanceWritingGigs.com**

  The name of this site pretty much says it all. Freelance-WritingGigs is a well-curated job board that gets updated twice a week—on Monday and on Friday—with some great new clients who pay well for writing.

- **PubLoft.com**

  This is a great place to find solid and well-paid freelance jobs from reliable clients. Additionally, with how the site is set up, you never have to actually interact with the client. The site promises that they will help ensure that freelancers won't have to find, sell, or manage their customers, and the gigs are well-paid too. The rates start at $150 per post, and the site will also help you strengthen your writing along the way, giving you plenty of room to work on your craft without the headaches of client management.

- **BloggingPro.com**

  Despite the name, you can find all kinds of different writing gigs on this site and even help other people start blogging. The site aggregates the best writing jobs, so it's easy to find and search through the site. This site is also completely free, which is a great plus!

- **Contently.com**

  This is a high-quality, agency-style platform that connects you directly with clients for some very well-paid freelance writing projects. Some clients pay as high as $600 to $1,600 per article depending on the length and scope. Clients usually come from the most successful brands and startups in the world. The catch, however, is that you must create a portfolio first, then their account management team will hand-select you for work. Still, the site provides solid freelance advice, and you receive a free portfolio as a creative freelancer.

- **FreelanceWriting.com**

  This is an easy one—you just sign up and they send you an email everyday with the latest freelance writing jobs. The best part is that it's totally free.

Designer Freelance Websites

These are the best websites for freelance design work where you get paid for excellent work without spending much time looking for jobs.

- **99Designs.com**

  This site has an interesting format—instead of publishing a job advertisement, the client would publish a contest. Designers submit their work as an application, the client chooses the one they like best, and that designer gets paid. The downside is that, if you don't win the contest, you don't get paid. However, you can still build up your portfolio using that work.

□ **Behance.net**

This isn't exactly a freelance job site, but it's still important because it helps designers showcase their work. By setting your work up on this site and choosing the right keywords, your work will come up higher in search engines when clients are looking to hire. The site is better than a personal website for showcasing your work and, for that reason, it's important to make use of it as a way to bring clients to you. Another benefit of this site is that you can receive feedback from other designers and potential clients on your work.

□ **Angel.co (AngelList)**

If you want to work for a startup company, then AngelList is for you. Startup companies of all kinds regularly search for talent on AngelList, and it can also help you to get your foot in the door for long-term employment.

□ **ArtWanted.com**

If your niche is graphic design or digital illustration, then you can put your work on this site. Potential clients browse the work by keywords and, if you choose your keywords well, you'll have a better chance of connecting with clients.

□ **DesignCrowd.com**

This site is similar to 99 Designs, but with fewer active designers. This site runs contests similar to 99 Designs, but they pay out lower amounts. However, both of these facts can help if you're a new designer. First of all, there is less competition as a result of the lower pay, meaning that you stand a better chance of being selected. It's a great way to build your starting portfolio.

□ **SmashingMagazine.com**

This is a great job board with resources for both developers and designers. It's easy to find freelancing jobs, even though you have to sort through the postings yourself.

Developer Freelance Websites

These sites are for developers, though people often lump designers and developers together, you can check out both this list and the one above.

□ **Gun.io**

If you believe you have the engineering skills to land freelance jobs with top companies like Tesla, Cisco, and Zappos, then this is the site for you. It's one of the best freelancing sites because of how they vet both companies that hire freelancers and the remote developers applying for gigs on the platform. If you get in on this site, you stand a greater chance of getting work since most freelance jobs are filled in less than 48 hours. That's a win for both the freelancer and the client.

□ **AskLorem.com**

This site is on the rise as one of the best sites for landing short-term freelance work for designing, building, and fixing websites. It's been featured in major publications like TechCrunch, The Wall Street Journal, and CNBC. Part of the reason it's appealing to clients is because there is no monthly fee to list freelance jobs, and most gigs pay between $25 and $250. One thing to keep in mind is that the Lorem team hand-vets the freelancers they allow on the platform, which means you'll have to apply to become one of their experts. However, once you're in, you can be assured a good chance of finding consistent work.

□ **Joomlancers.com**

This is the site for those who know their way around technology, as this site has a fast sign up process and allows you to start bidding on jobs almost immediately. The site focuses mostly on intermediate to advanced projects, so it will not be the place for beginners.

- **BetterTeam.com**

  This is the site for freelance programmers, developers, and even designers. It's also free to sign up.

- **10XManagement.com**

  This site is good for all sorts of tech freelancers—from developers to cybersecurity experts. If you have a niche tech specialty, this is the site for you. It's also good if you just have an interest and want to see what's possible.

- **Gigster.com**

  This is also a great site for various kinds of tech workers, with jobs on the site for software designers, web designers, and even app developers. There is a screening process, so you have to pass that first; however once you're in, the site uses AI to match you with projects. This is a great site if you have some experience.

Marketer Freelance Websites

A number of the sites already mentioned also list jobs for marketers; however, these specific sites are geared more toward marketing specializations.

- **PeoplePerHour.com**

  This is a great site for both marketers and SEO experts and software engineers. And, this site takes care of pretty much everything in the process, but they will only allow you to submit 15 free applications, before paying for more. You can browse for free though, and so, you can check it out to see if the site is right for you.

- **Remotive.io**

  This is a fairly standard board with a variety of categories, including marketing. It's easy to see when a new job has been posted, where it's located, and the specialty within marketing under which it falls. What's more is that this site is completely free to use.

- **Aquent.com**

  This company will make connections for you. The clients contact them, then they match the freelancer to the client. Their focus is mainly on marketing, but there are also a few tech and creative jobs as well.

Virtual Assistant Freelancer Websites

These include jobs like research, data entry, bookkeeping, and answering emails. Additionally, virtual assistants can specialize in a number of areas depending on their client's needs. These are some of the best sites for finding remote work:

- **BelaySolutions.com**

  This company offers virtual assistant work for their clients, and the work is always remote. It's definitely worth checking this site out to see if they have any openings within your specialty area.

- **TimeEtc.com**

  This site specializes in virtual assistant space, so it's great for those who are looking for this kind of work.

- **ClickWorker.com**

  This site has various tasks like writing, data entry, and researching. You have to take a quick assessment test, but once you get access to their job board, you will find that all kinds of companies post on their site. That includes large companies like PayPal. This is a great place to get started fast in virtual assistant freelancing.

- **MTurk.com (Amazon Mechanical Turk)**

  One of the big advantages of this site is that it allows you to find quick work fast. In fact, you can begin competing for jobs within an hour of getting on the site. There are also always numerous virtual assistant jobs, though one downside is that many of them don't pay that much.

- **VAnetworking.com**

  This is a great site for networking with other virtual assistants, and it has a great job board for finding freelance work. This site also provides resources appropriate for beginners and veterans alike.

- **AssistantMatch.com**

  This is another site that makes the connections for you. They will match your skills to the right client, though the pay isn't great for the beginners. Still, they do offer training for beginners, which can make it well worth your time.

Customer Support Freelance Websites

If you're into sales but don't like working in a store or driving to work, there are freelance and remote sales jobs available. The following sites can help you find them.

- **WeWorkRemotely.com**

  This site is for freelance workers of all kinds, along with numerous customer support jobs posted.

- **VirtualVocations.com**

  This site has a huge number of remote and freelance customer support jobs.

- **SupportDriven.com**

This is one of the few dedicated customer support freelance

job boards out there. It's definitely worth your time to check it out if customer support is part of your niche of freelance work.

As you can see, there are a variety of freelance job sites you can use to find work. You can also leverage your existing network and connections from previous jobs. The point is that there are many ways you can find freelance work. The sites we went over in this chapter can give you an idea of where to find jobs quickly, and many other sites are also growing on the internet. The work is there and, if you organize your freelance business well, you can find enough work to not only survive, but thrive.

Chapter Summary

In this chapter, you've learned about the types of freelance work available along with some of the best sites where you can find that work. We specifically covered the following topics:

- Finding freelance work that pays well.
- The specific kinds of freelance jobs pay well.
- Trending freelance jobs sites for both broad and specific types of work.

In the next chapter, we will go over what to avoid with freelance work.

---

[12] https://www.cnbc.com/2019/12/14/highest-paying-freelance-jobs-of-2020-where-you-earn-90000-or-more.html

Chapter **SIX**

FREELANCE OPPORTUNITIES— WHAT TO LOOK OUT FOR

Freelance work is not without its challenges, and there are pitfalls you'll want to avoid. It's important to understand the common mistakes before you get into this type of work.

Pitfalls to Avoid

While the coronavirus crisis may have pushed you into this type of work, you may find that you enjoy it in the end because of its flexibility, freedom, and various independent career paths. Therefore, to make sure you can achieve those ideals, watch out for the following pitfalls:

1. *Thinking like an employee*—it may be hard to get past the idea of traditional work culture. When you first start working for yourself, whether it's in freelance work or as an entrepreneur, it'll be easier to keep that 9 to 5 mentality. However, one of the worst mistakes you can make is limiting your hours while

waiting for freelance jobs to come your way. You will be responsible for marketing yourself, updating your own skills, negotiating and monitoring for your services, and prioritizing projects to meet deadlines. That means working long hours frequently to keep your business running smoothly. Nevertheless, if you put in the hours, you'll soon find that you have steady work and repeat clients that will take a lot of that pressure off. You'll also find yourself getting more efficient with your skills, and you will be able to finish your jobs faster.

2. *Simply following directions*—you may be used to doing this in your traditional job, but now you are not an employee, you are a consultant, partner, and skilled expert at what you do. In some languages, a freelancer is translated as an independent expert. Your clients provide you with the rationale, background information, and parameters for the project, but it is you who brings the knowledge, expertise, and a new perspective to the job.

You need to think of yourself as equal to your client. The two of you are collaborating on the project, and you are taking the initiative. You have to take the bull by the horns and be ready to advise your client on what you know works for the project. Your opinion is part of the value you bring to the client.

Employees often feel that their company does not care much about their opinion, but the latter often does listen. Your opinion really matters and must be clearly articulated. If you are not sure, you still want to mention the possibilities to the client. If you know something is probable or that a particular result is dependent on factors that neither of you can control, you need to explain that to the client. They will appreciate your candor.

3. *Scattershot approach to finding clients and accepting every project*—it may be tempting to take any project that comes your way, particularly at first, but this is a mistake. Likewise, you also **93**

need to systematize the way you find clients. You would start by identifying your ideal client, getting your portfolio and website together, then approaching only those clients for whom you know you can produce good work products. While the online job boards can get you started, referrals, word-of-mouth advertising, and your personal and professional networks will be the best ways to find clients.

4. *Accepting low pay*—it's easy to fall into the trap of accepting less pay for a variety of reasons. You might like the client or think you need the experience, but the reality is that you only need to accept a price that really reflects your true value. If you want to make a sustainable living, you'll need to charge what you're worth. However, if a dumping price can give you a higher chance of landing jobs with a client for your standard prices, you can use that strategy. In addition, during the coronavirus crisis, it may become difficult to find a sustainable job; therefore, you may need to reconsider your standard prices.

5. *Poor communication*—you should never take anything for the obvious. When you are working with a client, you need to have crystal clear communication, so you fully understand what they truly want. That will be to your advantage, because you don't want to produce something they are not satisfied with—that will only result in bad reviews. Communicate early, clearly, and often with your clients. Respond promptly to any questions or messages they send and make sure they know from the outset how to contact you and when you can be reached. The best practice is to document everything agreed to, along with the basis for and results of each communication. Misunderstanding happens frequently, and you can help avoid that by documenting your understanding of the communication meticulously as you go. Then, you can send notes from a meeting or after a communication detailing your interpretation of the event. Once the client confirms them, they also become bound to them.

6. *Failing to suggest another project or losing client connections—* your current or past clients are great possible future clients. So, when the current project is coming to an end, if it is appropriate to do so, suggest another possible project. If a new project isn't a current possibility at the moment, be sure to keep in contact with that client so you're the first on their mind when a new potential project comes up.

   Send them emails on occasion showing that you care about them. Clients will remember those who stood with them during the coronavirus crisis. They also prefer to have a pool of proven freelancers—when they have an opportunity, it becomes convenient for them to send you an email asking whether you are available for another job.

   Also, when you propose the first contract, don't include an end date. That way, the next time the client sends you an offer, it can become a contract once you accept it. The client will value you more from the first day because they will see you want to build a long-term relationship over making a quick buck.

7. *Missed deadlines—*this mistake will kill your freelance business very quickly. If you want those great reviews and word-of-mouth advertising that will bring you more clients, make sure to meet your deadlines. If, for some reason, you can't meet a deadline, be sure to communicate with the client and ensure they understand the situation. However, that should be the exception, not the rule. When you are responsible for missing the deadline, offer a price discount or an extra value to the client. They will see that you are being responsible and want to provide added value to the client. Meeting deadlines is a critical part of professional behavior and, if you miss deadlines repeatedly, your clients will go elsewhere, so take great pains to avoid this error. **95**

8. ***Getting angry with a client*—**it's true that clients can be exasperating, but you should never get angry with them. Blow off steam elsewhere, find someone to vent to, or simply walk away from the computer or telephone until you calm down. Remember the old adage: *"the customer is always right."* That applies to clients too. You need to maintain a professional attitude at all times, or you will lose clients fast. As a freelancer or an entrepreneur, keep the highest professional standards and never compromise, regardless of the client's behavior.

9. ***Putting all your eggs in one basket*—**you don't want to have just one or two clients because it is always a possibility that a client can no longer pay you for an ongoing project or you could lose a client for reasons outside your control. It is vital as a freelance worker to have multiple sources of income, and building up several months' worth of savings to get through lean time is ideal.

10. ***Taking on too many projects at once*—**this is the other side of the coin to the point above. You need more than just one or two sources of income, but taking on too many jobs will reduce the quality of your work, which may result in bad reviews. Nobody can work crazy hours for very long. You will become efficient as a freelancer, but that also means that, after 8 hours of work, you will get tired. If this situation occurs too often, you will eventually burn out. Remember that flexibility is an advantage of self-employment, so if you have too many projects at once, take a step back and work on fewer projects. Make those decisions strategically. If you have to choose between two job offers, select the one with the larger long-term benefit, which will likely be a recurring client.

Clients to Avoid

Aside from making certain mistakes as you work for clients, there are also clients that you are wise to avoid. Although you may think accepting every project that comes your way is the best way to do your business, there are some clients who will never be satisfied or will constantly make your life miserable when you work with them. To help you stay productive and enjoy your work, here is a list of clients it's best to avoid:

◻ **"I don't know what I want"**

If the client doesn't really know what they want, you will both end up frustrated. Before you accept a client, you should discuss their goals in detail so you can make sure they have a clear idea of what they hope to accomplish. Their goals should also be specific. For example, merely saying, "I want to increase web traffic," is not specific enough. What does that mean? By how much? In what time frame? Once you have a better understanding of what the client wants to achieve, make sure you can deliver it. If the scope is something you can't guarantee or deliver on, be honest and tell the client you may not be right for what they want to do. Trying to take on something you can't deliver will only result in frustration and bad reviews.

On the other hand, your client may not be an expert on web traffic, thus wants to hire you. In this case, it would be your responsibility—and a great opportunity—to offer one or more solutions. If the client is not willing to agree on specific conditions, do not enter such a relationship because both sides will be disappointed.

◻ **Houdini**

This is the type of client who doesn't answer their emails or phone, and sometimes completely disappears altogether. It can delay your progress and cause big problems when you need to make important transactions, like getting paid. With such clients, whenever you need a quick answer to a question, it can become frustrating if your work is held up while you wait to get that answer.

This kind of client is hard to identify from the start, but if you start seeing this pattern within your first few interactions, you may need to let the client know that their behavior is not something you can work with. It's worth cutting them loose if they don't plan to work with you to produce good, timely work. If you received the client through a freelance web page, your fee for the milestone should be secured. However, if you have a direct contract with the client, make sure there are clauses ensuring you will get paid for a milestone, even if you could not finish it due the client's lack of availability.

◻ **The Barterer**

Exchanging services has its place in the freelance world; for example, it can be a great way to partner with a new client. However, you have to be sure everyone involved is benefiting from the deal. Clients who want to exchange services or products you don't need or want aren't really offering you something of value, so don't make those deals. Since you can't barter to pay your bills, this should be the exception rather than the rule.

◻ **Mr. or Ms. Wrong**

This client has gone through many freelancers and, just like a bad boy or party girl, there's probably a good reason for it. You might think you can change the client or that you'll finally be the one to satisfy them, but the reality is, if so many others have failed before you, it's unlikely you'll be the one to make this client happy. In addition, doing lots of work for a client who will never be happy will be unlikely to land you a good review.

Thus, before you agree to work with a client, learn a bit about their past experience with other professionals. Ask them about other freelancers they've worked with, what made them look for someone else, and consider whether those past freelancers are people you know who have good track records. If they do, the problem may be with the client and not with the freelancers. Some freelancing platforms like Upwork show reviews the client gave on the freelancer and vice versa. If any side has three stars or less, read those comments carefully and be warned if the client's average score is below 4 stars.

One of the most important things to remember as a freelance worker is that you have valuable services to offer clients, so don't sell yourself short. Don't accept every job that comes your way, avoid accepting clients who are never satisfied or are micromanagers, and charge appropriately for your services. The services you are offering are valuable, and you are partnering with your clients—you are *not* their employee. Basically, when you make the switch to freelance work, you have to adjust your mindset to recognize that you are a general manager of your freelance business now. You will serve your client as an equal by providing valuable services or products. Once you adjust your thinking, you can then achieve a successful, fulfilling life in the gig economy.

Chapter Summary

WORK
FROM
HOME

In this chapter, we've looked at some of the more common pitfalls you can make as a freelance worker, and we've also discussed certain types of clients you should avoid. Specifically, we covered the following topics:

- Common freelance mistakes.
- Changing your mindset.
- Professional behavior.
- Communication.
- You are an equal to the client and will provide professional services.

In the next chapter, we will cover the various forms of online and remote entrepreneurial opportunities.

Chapter SEVEN

ONLINE ENTREPRENEURSHIP OPPORTUNITIES

IN this chapter, we will be going over the best online business and entrepreneurial opportunities you can partake in. It's helpful first to understand the difference between online entrepreneurship and business opportunities compared to freelancing work. While it is advisable to set up any freelance work you do as a business, there is a difference between working as a freelancer and starting your own online business.

With the former, you have clients telling you their requirements. That differs from starting your own business, in that you will be offering specific, pre-identified services or products to customers. That means you will have to define customer needs and determine how you can meet those needs. This is something that may entail an initial financial investment, and it will most certainly require a time investment to get set up.

Another difference is in the risk and opportunities associated with freelancing versus owning your own business. Freelancers don't really risk losing their businesses and they don't have to make any big investment that they have to worry about losing either. On the other hand, their earnings are limited by their hourly price and the time they can work. Business owners can lose all their investments and even the entire business, but have no upper limit on how much they can earn. As long as their product or service is in demand, they can become millionaires.

The higher limit with businesses can be an exciting thought. It is also one of the better ways to achieve a dream of financial freedom, better lifestyle for you and your family, and the opportunity to do something you really enjoy. So, how would you get started? The great thing about an online business is that all you need to get started is a phone, computer, and internet connection; the hard part is coming up with a good business idea. Such involves the consideration of at least the three following things:

1. You want it to be something you enjoy doing.

2. You want it to be something you do well.

3. It needs to be in demand; in other words, it should be something people will pay for. This last point is the most important consideration you should take. If you have identified a high demand for something you don't enjoy or aren't good at producing, then you can hire freelancers who will do that job for you. It will be more expensive and maybe not as enjoyable as some other jobs, but you can still earn a lot with a good business idea.

To help you decide on the business that will work best for you, we will be looking at some of the best options in this category. These will include easy startup business ideas, along with more profitable and in-demand options.

Great Online Business Ideas

The following business opportunities are categorized according to their general business type. Many of these businesses overlap with freelancing, and freelancing can be a stepping stone to starting your own online business. As a freelance worker, you learn to navigate a number of personal risks, make important decisions, and advertise your services. These skills all prepare you for business ownership, thus if you don't think you're ready to be an entrepreneur yet, you can start with freelancing. The main difference between freelancing and owning your own business is that, as a business owner, you would decide which activities you want to perform yourself and which to outsource. Therefore, have an open mind—it is normal to outsource accounting and tax matters to a professional, so don't be afraid to delegate other tasks as needed. You merely cannot delegate the ultimate responsibility for the business, which is no different from what any other CEO would do.

You are the CEO or managing director of your business. You may be your sole employee in some cases, but you can outsource work as appropriate when you are the business owner. The CEO in a large company wouldn't do the work associated with production; rather, they would make decisions and ensure the necessary work is all completed. In a small or one-person company, the CEO may have to do certain work; however, their main responsibility is to make good business decisions. The CEO should outsource all activities unless they can do them very well. The CEO must also take responsibility for any poor decisions made within and around their business. We all make mistakes, but the CEO must be mature enough to learn from their own mistakes.

A number of online businesses may seem like freelance jobs—though they may be providing freelance services, there are various important differences between a business that use freelance labor and selling services. Though a business may start out as an individual who was both doing work in and running the business, that would often change quickly as the business grows. Many businesses that provide online services use several freelance workers to provide their clients with high quality services. They connect the client with the freelancer, then pay the freelancer once the product or service is completed. Thus, with these online business opportunities, though you may start out small with just yourself working, the focus would be to grow your business to where you would be outsourcing the lion's share of the work you're doing for your clients.

Publishing Businesses

If you're running a publishing business, then you're producing content. That can be done for direct sales profits, such as with publishing and selling a book, or indirectly by producing a blog ultimately designed to generate, for example, an email list of potential customers.

- *Blogging services*—right now, it's easier than ever before to start a blog. If you know what you're doing, it can be a great source of income. The key is to monetize it, which you can do in a few ways. If you are selling a product or service on a website, your blog can help to generate an email list when offering your products or services. You can even outsource the blog writing to qualified freelancers. Another way to earn money with a blog is to combine it with affiliate marketing— you may go check out the description of that under "Marketing Businesses," below, but this is essentially when you market someone else's products or services and earn a commission on the sales.

  If you're diligent in your efforts, blogging can become quite profitable—in some cases, bloggers can make more than 105

$50,000 per year. There are several sites where you can create a blog for a minimal investment, and many of these blog sites will provide you with the tools to help increase the traffic to your site, including keyword identifiers to help your site rank higher in the search engines. However, as the business owner, it's also possible to outsource the site management to freelancers.

Blogging by itself is often done for free and does not generate large income, though it's still really a great way to get an online business started. If you can successfully attract people to your site, those same people may become your future customers. There is, however, another way to do business in blogging—you can create a business that provides blogs to clients for publication on their websites. With this model, you would contract out blog-writing services by pairing a blogger with the client. Again, if you're just starting out, that could mean you're initially writing blogs for several clients, but you can start hiring other freelancers to write the blogs under your name as your business grows.

◻ *Self-publish a book on Amazon*—no matter if you're looking to write the Great American Novel or pay a freelancer to write it, Amazon makes publishing easy. There are a number of guides out there that can help you to both write the book and have it actually generate income. In fact, platforms like Amazon provide writers and publishers with tools that allow them to search a topic of interest and view the selling success of other books in that category.

There are two ways you can go with a self-published book: the first is fiction books that people enjoy reading, whereas the second is nonfiction books that people read to learn about specific topics. Both can be lucrative, but it's important that they are written to appeal to their respective audiences, as well as marketed appropriately. You can, once again, outsource the writing to a freelance writer, and you can also outsource the marketing task. As the business owner, you will need to oversee that each part of the process is done in accordance with your business model. If you're thinking of going this route, it's also advisable to continue and publish several books while they are mutually supporting sales. They don't have to be long, and if you market them correctly, they can bring in significant amounts of money each month.

Marketing is the key to generating high sales of your books. It's a great idea to run a promotion in the first week and advertise to your email list and across all your social media platforms to generate higher sales. If you can generate high enough sales in the first week on a platform like Amazon, they will then start to help you promote the book, which is how to start really making money as a writer or self-publisher.

- *Copywriting*—This is both the art and science of getting people to take action on a cause, and can be either written or spoken. Copywriters can write sales pages, emails, and blog content. It's also a lucrative field if you become good enough at it. As a business owner, you can supply copywriting services to a number of potential clients—that is, anyone who advertises—and you can outsource the writing, so you can concentrate on attracting clients and finding highly talented freelancers to write for them.

- *Technical writing*—Technical writing is a solid field in which to start a business. It is projected to grow faster than average at approximately 8% between now and 2028[13] (U.S. Bureau of Labor Statistics, 2019), making it a great business opportunity. Technical writers write instruction manuals for things like your TV, building a coffee stand, how your car operates, among other jobs. If you start a business in this area, you will likely be able to find numerous clients with writing you can again outsource to qualified freelancers.

- ***Resume and cover letter writing***—this field can generate more than $1000 per month in income. You would structure the service in accordance with the types of clients and their needs. An entry-level resume would be at the lower end at around $400, but an executive resume or that which is specific to a particular field would cost much more. Customers would also be willing to pay more for a quick turnaround[14] (Truex, 2018). If you can attract the clients to your business, you can maintain a stable of writers who can generate solo resumes and resume packages containing cover letters and, often, follow-up letters.

Marketing Businesses

These are businesses in which you would help someone sell their products or services. Depending on the type of marketing you offer, you could earn either a commission on the sales or a fee for creating effective ads.

- ***Affiliate marketing***—this involves promoting someone else's product and earning a commission as you do so. There are a few ways you can follow through with this service, the first being promoting products like ebooks, memberships, video series, among other informational products. The provision ranges between 5% and 50% percent, or it is a fixed amount. It has low barriers to entry, and it's easy to find products to promote.

  Another way to do this is to partner with an affiliate program. Amazon, Commission Junction, and Clickbank are three such programs you can consider. They offer easy entrances into affiliate marketing, and you can affiliate quickly with numerous well-known companies that pay good commissions. There are millions of profitable products to choose from too. It is helpful to have some knowledge of SEO and copywriting if you want to get into affiliate marketing; however, as a business owner, you can still outsource these skills while you work on finding clients and sales channels.

◻ *SEO*—SEO stands for Search Engine Optimization, which refers to getting websites or blog posts to rank higher in search engines such as Google. The key is understanding the search terms that people use when looking for products, services, or information. The higher a website ranks, the more traffic it receives and revenue the owner makes. This is a highly-valued skill in internet marketing, but it can be challenging since search engines like Google frequently change their algorithms, along with some of the rules. Therefore, if your business specializes in SEO services, you will need to make sure you're always up-to-date on the newest strategies.

◻ *Facebook advertising*—as Facebook continues to grow, businesses are beginning to spend more on Facebook advertisements, but many of them don't actually understand Facebook ads. That will be where your business comes in. If you are, can become, or hire a Facebook ad specialist, you can offer to create effective Facebook ads for them as a service. If you don't know how to do it yourself, it's something you can learn fairly quickly, or you can outsource that work as the business owner. Like any advertising service, the potential for a business to earn a good income is quite high when you assist clients in driving their measurable outcomes, save them time, and provide them with proven expertise.

◻ *Lead generation*—leads are the lifeblood of businesses. Lead generation is the process of attracting and converting prospective customers into individuals interested in a business' product or service. Businesses are always looking to generate new leads, and, if you create a business that can assist with that, you can then make a good income. This is probably the single most important aspect of a business; therefore, if you can connect your clients with a good lead generator, they will pay well for that service. **109**

Sales Companies

There are a number of different ways you can engage in online sales. These business opportunities can help you earn a good income with little overhead or initial investment.

- *Set up an e-commerce site*—for many e-commerce markets, you're competing against old school business people who may not have much experience in online marketing. That can give you a distinct advantage, but it does require some hard work. The first stepping stone would be that you have to stand out among hundreds of thousands of other e-commerce websites. However, if you can find the right niche and execute the appropriate marketing techniques, you can have success with your e-commerce store.

  To do that, you'll want to brainstorm ideas for a profitable market, and some strategic keyword research will help you here. The next thing to consider is whether the product is a high or low margin product. Low margin products would require a high turnover to generate good profit. The margin is the difference between the selling price and purchase price, and it must cover all your expenses and generate a certain profit. Finally, you will want to ensure the product is something within a growth market. If it's already passed its peak, you should look at something else, preferably an industry on the upswing.

  Once you have the product, you'll need to create a good-looking store quickly. This can be done with a minimal investment, and you don't have to be a coder to do it. Shopify is one such user-friendly site, and its 30-day free trial won't have you spending a dime to get started.

- *Sell products on eBay*—this may be considered old-school now, but you can still make lots of money selling on its platform. You can start by buying something simple, like clothing on sale, then list it on eBay for a higher price. If it sells, you can then reinvest the profit by buying more items to continue making more profit. It requires a bit of strategy, but it can still be a profitable online business.

- *Buy and flip domains*—this is similar to those realtors who buy and flip real estate, except you're doing it in the virtual world. Just like with realtors, you would buy domains—perhaps fixing them up a bit—then sell them for a profit. It can generate pretty good money, particularly if you try to get ahead of trends and purchase hot item domains.

Information for Sale

With these kinds of online businesses, you would basically be monetizing your expertise. There are a couple of ways you can do that.

- *Create online courses*—there are a few different platforms where you can do this. Udemy.com is a site where you can create the course and earn a percentage of the profits. You can also earn a greater percentage for students who find your course through your own advertising. You don't have to have a PhD to offer a course—you can create a course on, for example, how to change the oil in your car or how to paint a mountain landscape, all without formal education on the topic. Anything you have expertise on can be the subject matter for one of these courses. You can also self-publish a text to go along with your course to create two sources of income, while marketing each.

- *Coaching*—coaching is a hot, new trend these days, and there also exist several kinds of coaches, including life coaches, health coaches, dating coaches, among others. For this kind of business, you would need expertise in some topic, along with video conferencing capabilities through platforms like Skype, Zoom, or Google Hangouts. Essentially, you and your client 111 would be calling daily, weekly, or monthly depending on the preference, and you would help them with the topic of coaching you offer. It's also helpful for marketing if you have a blog on your coaching topic or publish an ebook to generate another income stream.

- *Start a podcast*—podcasts are great revenue generators. Once again, if you have expertise in some area, you can start a podcast in which you discuss the topic, invite guests for interviews, and take questions from listeners. As you grow your podcast, you can then begin to offer paid sponsorships and/or sell your own products and services. By earning the trust of your listeners, they will become much more likely to buy what you're selling.

- *Become a YouTuber*—YouTube videos are all the rage these days, so if you like being in front of the camera, you can speak directly to your audience and build a lucrative online business. Among topics to choose from, you could pitch products, voice your opinions, educate people, react to games or other videos, and much more. Your revenue comes from advertising in your videos and affiliated sales. Along with that, and with no more than just your smartphone, you can produce and upload videos starting today, though many YouTubers will tell you it's worth the investment to have a good microphone and stage setup.

Design and Development Businesses

If you're a technology nerd, these businesses can be a way to make considerable profits. There are a number of different opportunities available in this niche.

- *App development*—mobile apps continue to be as popular as ever, and this could be a lucrative option if you have a cool idea for a fun or useful app. It's helpful to have coding knowledge for this option; however, if you don't, you can still probably find someone who does who would be willing to collaborate on creating your app. Because there are so many apps out there right now, you'll want to validate your idea first before you invest any time or money in it.

- *Web developer*—this is someone who can build a website from the bottom up. You'll definitely need to choose a development framework suitable for the type and features of web pages you want to create. It can take time to learn, but it's worth the effort because this niche pays well and the demand is continuously growing.

- *Graphic design*—graphic designers are visual communicators. They design web pages, sale pages, logos, and any other polished and professional graphics. When you see a web page that is well-organized and easy to use, that's thanks to a graphic designer. To be good at this job, you don't necessarily have to be able to draw, have a college degree, or even have a fancy computer. You do, however, need to be someone who thinks visually, and you'll need to specialize in a specific form of design or topic. You will be creating a good user experience with graphical user interface features.

- *Build niche sites*—niche sites target a specific audience. For example, a niche site would not just be a site about photography, but it would also be a site about landscape photography. By targeting that specific niche, you would likely receive a higher rank on Google for keyword searches, then, of course, you would want to turn that traffic into earnings. That can be done by either selling your own products or through affiliate marketing. This type of business has a really high workload; however, if you can create a good niche site, it can bring in an extra $500 in monthly earnings or more.

113

Other Online Businesses

The following are several potentially lucrative online businesses.

- **Consulting**—if you have specific knowledge that is helpful to other businesses, you can get paid as a consulting firm for them. You'll have to be able to apply the knowledge, skills, and experience you have to help solve problems for their company. Compared to freelance consultancy, you can hire a team or use professional freelancers to offer complex services and scale the business.

- **Instagram sponsorships**—if taking photos and building a huge following on Instagram is your dream, you can find some sponsorship opportunities that will pay you to do just that. If, for example, your account is about all things fitness, you could sponsor products like supplements or gym equipment, which could then make you a lot of money if you're a social media influencer.

- **Tech support**—here, you would be offering your skills as a tech whiz, which is a valuable skill in this day and age. You can work with big companies or one-on-one with clients. Either way, you will likely gain lots of business in this field.

- **Accounting, processing documents, and administrative services**—the focus of these firms would be to prepare financial documents, provide bookkeeping services, provide document processing services, and offer a variety of administrative services to any number of clients.

This list of options is by no means exhaustive, but they are areas where you can get your remote business set up and start making money relatively quickly. These are business opportunities that will not only allow you to survive the coronavirus crisis, but also realize your dreams of a major lifestyle change fully.

You can make money in a way that also gives you the freedom

to live life on your own terms. You can also love what you do and have plenty of time for family, friends, and fun. Next, I will be taking you through how to get set up in an online entrepreneurial business.

Chapter Summary

In this chapter, we've gone over various entrepreneurial opportunities available online. Specifically, I've covered the following topics:

- Difference between an online business and online freelancing.
- Discovering the type of online business you'd like to create.
- Different categories of online businesses.
- Specific kinds of online businesses you can create quickly with minimal cash investment.

In the next chapter, we'll be going over how to start up your online business.

WORK
FROM
HOME

Chapter EIGHT

ONLINE ENTREPRENEURSHIP– GETTING SET UP

WHILE it might seem daunting to start a business, starting up an online business is actually much easier than you may think, despite it requiring some forethought. It also requires a fundamental change in mindset. Before I talk about that, however, let me give you a definition for an online business. Essentially, an online business requires that you market and advertise it, attract customers, process payments, deliver products, and manage all the other components online for the most part.

Another important factor for any business owner to consider—not just those online—is that you have to change your mindset. As I discussed with making the change from employee to freelancer, there is another fundamental shift when making the leap to the business owner. If you're creating your own business, you have to identify your customers and their needs, then create products or services that address those needs. You also need to be able to deliver in a way that gives them the most value for their money. You are no longer simply an employee or even a self-employed freelancer being directed by a boss or client; you are now the business owner. Therefore, you—and only you—are responsible for your own success or failure. It's important that you think about it from that perspective. With this in mind, let's look at how you can get your new business up and running.

Step #1: Research

The first thing you need to do is research the market for your specific niche. Make sure you learn what works and what doesn't so you don't make the same mistakes others have made. You need to look into how you can monetize your ideas and passions. Will your decided business work? Is there a market for it? What does it take to monetize it? You will want to learn as much as you can about your idea to give your business the best chance for success.

Step #2: Identifying Your Audience and Your Competition

You need to know who your clients are and identify how you plan to help them. You need to ask yourself the following questions:

1. What customers' problem does my business solve?

2. Who needs my service?

3. Why should they pick my business over the competition?

One way to figure out if people will be interested in what you are offering is to use a keyword tool and see how frequently people search for your service. Google's keyword tool will return information on the number of searches conducted each month worldwide. Thus, it's a good idea to direct your attention toward niches with between 10,000 and 50,000 searches each month. The keyword tool also lets you know if the competition in that market is high, medium, or low, and you can also insert your keywords in a Google search and see how many results are returned. Researching keywords will give you a great idea of the level of competition. 119

Step #3: Write a Business Plan

It is imperative that you have a plan and stick to it as much as possible. With a business plan, you'll want to, once again, identify the problem your business solves, your target market, and how you can reach them. Furthermore, you'll want to identify your startup costs, so you know the costs for getting the business up and running.

You'll also want to determine your pricing models and business expenses. If you plan to outsource work, you'll want to identify how you will find those freelancers and figure out a price range for their services, which should be included in your business expenses. With your expenses identified, you can then determine the amount you'll be charging for your services or product.

Make sure you also identify the risks, obstacles, and competition you will be encountering, along with your strategies for overcoming all these problems. At the very end, describe what success looks like. This last part of your business plan is critical, as it helps keep you focused and motivated. Changes will be necessary to the overall plan in some cases; however, you should document them to keep track.

Step #4: Name, Domain, and Website

Just as you did with the freelance business entity, you will want to choose a name, purchase a domain—which is not very expensive—and set up a website. At this stage, you will need to create your business entity. If you're setting up your business in the United States, the same business structures discussed earlier apply; although, for starting a business, an LLC or C-Corps will be your best options, particularly because you will be outsourcing work. Those entities will give your company the best potential for growth. There are different models in other countries, and you'll want to investigate the options in your area if you're located outside the US.

You also need to have a website where you can direct potential clients, build email lists, post blogs, and offer your services. For that, it will be best to have a domain name that's easy to remember, which will make it easier for people to find it. Your website will be essential to your business' success and, for that reason, it may be worth hiring a website designer. You will want to get started on the right foot, so it's best to make sure everything is as perfect as it can possibly be before you launch your business. Hiring a website designer can help ensure your online presence is attractive and client-friendly, giving prospective clients a good first impression.

Step #5: Finances

If you need startup money, make sure you save enough to cover your expenses and provide a cushion until you can begin to make a profit. You will also want to make sure you have a bank account set up to handle your money as it comes in and need to pay for expenses.

Step #6: Sign Up for an Email Delivery Service

As long as it's stood, email is still the most productive way to promote and market your business online. These services take care of sending emails to your clients and prospective clients. One example of this kind of service is MailChimp, which is a leader in the market. Your account on their service is free, which is a great place to start. They also have an exceptionally user-friendly website and provide training videos to help you make sure your business is a success.

Step #7: Marketing Your Business

Building a website isn't enough—you have to attract traffic to your website. There are two main ways you can do this: the free way and the paid way. The free way involves a greater time investment before seeing results, whereas the paid way accelerates the income. The free way would include generating email lists and making use of your social media platforms, which can work, even if it does take more time.

If you want quicker results, you will want to advertise your business online, which can bring you traffic instantly. There are a number of different ways you can do this—one that is often a great place to start is Google AdWords. It can get you great results, though you do need to understand how to use it, or you will end up generating more losses than wins. Your page will rank at the top of Google searches, and you would pay for every click that directs users to your page. It might also be worthwhile to outsource that to a marketing pro. If you can afford to do that, you should receive strong and fast results.

Step #8: Network

Even though you're taking your business online, it doesn't necessarily mean that you would stop being part of your professional community. You can join a forum within your niche, for example, and that can be a great source of information and inspiration. You can comment on blogs within your niche, engage in Twitter conversations, join a Facebook or LinkedIn group, or even make professional friends on StumbleUpon or YouTube. This kind of networking gets you out there and makes other professionals aware of your presence, which can bring in referrals and ideas for making your business even
better.

Step #9: Plan Your Launch

When you launch your new business, you will want to make as big a splash as you can. Thus, it's a great idea to plan promotions, such as a special pricing for the first 100 visitors to your site or during the first week of business. Promotions can generate a lot of traffic that will hopefully include return customers. Treat the initial discounts as an investment that can turn many visitors into paying customers. State it clearly that the discount is for a limited time only. Announce your launch date and time, along with any promotions anywhere you can think of—social media platforms, chatrooms, group forums, and, of course, on your company's website. Try to get the word out to as many people as possible. The bigger a splash you make in the beginning, the more traffic you can generate for those email lists.

Step #10: Don't Stop Growing and Improving

Just because you've launched your business or even achieved a few of your goals, it doesn't mean there's time to rest on your laurels. It's a never-ending journey where you are constantly learning new ways to improve your skills and grow your business; running and maintaining takes persistence and commitment. If you're not growing, then your business is dying, so don't stop learning new ways to market and promote it. You want to track everything, optimize your website, and get more conversions. A *conversion* is when you get a potential client to take an action you want, like signing up for email updates or clicking on a button to add your product to their cart. To be truly successful, you have to keep the game going. That will be how you build the business and lifestyle you've always dreamed about.

By following these ten steps, you can quickly get your online business up and running. It's relatively easy to do, and it can be done with no initial investment other than your time, though the road is easier if you have some money to invest. Once you've gotten your business up and running, you will be well on your way to that rewarding life in which you control your destiny.

Chapter Summary

In this chapter, we've gone through the main steps to take for setting up your online business. Specifically, we have covered the following topics:

- Researching your niche.
- Identifying your clients, competition, and startup needs.
- Getting your business entity created and setting up your online presence.
- Finding clients, marketing, and drawing traffic to your website.
- Planning your launch, networking, and maintaining growth.

In the next chapter, we will cover the most realistic online businesses and go over examples of successful online models.

Chapter **NINE**

ONLINE ENTREPRENEURIAL EXAMPLES AND SITES

There are lots of great online business opportunities, and the reality is that you can launch and make good money with an online business for very little or even no capital investment. If you understand how online marketing works, or you're a whiz at social media, you'll likely find setting up and running an online business pretty easy. So, what kinds of businesses are the most likely to make good money right now?

Entrepreneurial Winners

There are a number of business opportunities that are trending now. Let's take a look at why they work and why they're likely to continue being winning models.

◻ Chatbot Business

With the popularity of Facebook and other social media platforms, people have grown accustomed to chatting with friends and family, even if they're located on the other side of the world. That is precisely why chatbots powered by artificial intelligence (AI) present a great opportunity for entrepreneurs looking to help businesses automate and reduce the manpower it takes to chat with customers.

Businesses across all spectrums are taking advantage of this kind of technology. Numerous platforms—such as Manychat and ChattyPeople—are cropping up and taking the complexity out of building a chatbot. In fact, there is now a stampede of people wanting to launch chatbots to automate at least some of their sales and marketing efforts. In addition, while chatbots may help make businesses more efficient, there's also an opportunity for you to get rich selling these businesses the tools to do just that.

◻ Subscription Box Business

This is one business that was developed years ago, but has seen a revival in the age of the internet. Subscription boxes are a marketing strategy that involves the recurring delivery of niche products. They target a wide range of customers, even though they cater to very specific needs.

The subscription box business starts with a basic level of items the customer orders on a recurring basis. When the customer places an order, they are directed into a sales funnel that includes numerous upsells called add-ons. It's an effective strategy, and the subscription box industry saw a roughly 30 times increase between 2013 and 2016[15] (Adams 2019). The typical visitor to a subscription box site is in their early 40s. This model will work for many years of recurring sales that can make you more than $75,000 per year.

◻ **Ad Management Business**

Now, more than ever, it's all about the advertising. There's a lot of competition for customers on the internet, and you can sell your services to businesses that are hungry for people like you if you have a strong understanding of how to drive paid traffic and optimize conversions. Knowing the specifics of marketing, redirecting and improving conversions, and the ebb and flow of sales funnels can make your business a hot commodity.

Consider the fact that digital ad spending in the US is expected to surpass two-thirds of total media spending by 2023, and it is already exceeding traditional advertising[16] (eMarketer, 2019). That represents an explosive growth of online ads, and the internet is really still in its infancy. If you can capitalize on this industry, you can build a formidable online business.

◻ **SEO Business**

Search engine optimization is another growing business that relates to marketing. Paid ads are growing at an astounding rate, but if a business can rank higher in search engines like Google, they will be more competitive and lucrative.

Roughly 40% of people click on the first search results that pop up in their browser, and the first page accounts for 91% of the search share (Adams, 2019). Because of that, businesses will pay good money to someone who can help rank their business higher in search engine results. If your business can provide that service, you can easily capitalize on this industry.

◻ **Webinar Business**

Webinars are one of the better ways to sell online. The audience is already engaged in the product, thus they are ready and willing to purchase what you're offering. The best part is that you don't have to be selling your own product for you to make a fortune in this industry.

The best way to get started is to find a product that you truly believe in, then build an excellent webinar to promote it. There are even software programs that can help you build an entire webinar, including copy for ads and swipes. If you're good at it, you can build a lucrative business as a sales affiliate.

Business Coaching

If you have a good understanding of the forces that drive purchases, you can make a great income as a business coach. There is a growing number of business coaches hired by entrepreneurs and business owners to help them find their way in the world of commerce in general, and this is now a growing field for online businesses.

The key to this field is to offer an incredible value to your clients upfront, then they will pay you for the execution of those ideas. You want to analyze your client's business to understand where it is at the moment and where they hope to take it in the future. Once you know that, you can help them devise how to get where they want to go. To be really successful in this industry, you will need some proof that you're good. Focus on getting a few customers and helping them succeed; then, you can use their testimonials to justify charging better rates.

Online Learning

This is one area where the opportunity is growing, given the current pandemic. Online learning portals are still evolving, and a growing number of students don't want to study in conventional ways. Thus, the modern mobile lifestyle is a perfect fit for online learning platforms. You don't need to develop a university platform, though that is an option. You can, however, develop online vocational learning platforms or other sub-niches like continuing education for professionals or online business training programs. Either direction will build your revenue.

Online Grocery and Foods

This is another opportunity that has been highlighted in the current pandemic. It's also been growing in popularity among busy people who don't have time to go grocery shopping. In fact, busy people are target clients for this growing industry. If you have a talent for driving customers to your business and can maintain good relations with vendors, this can be a successful business for you. You can start out small and increase your services and products as your business grows.

Baby Rompers Online Store Business

This is a great online business idea, particularly for stay-at-home parents. Baby rompers are dresses for babies, and nearly everyone has fallen in love with them by this point. They show a substantial search volume, and you could use baby rompers as a trending product if you want to open an online store. In addition, you can add a variety of baby clothes to help your store become a one-stop-shop for busy parents. Helping parents reduce their load can mean a big boon for your business, and you won't need a lot of experience to get started.

Online Customer Engagement Platform

Customer service is one area that is vital to any business, and they are always looking for ways to attract more users. If you are someone who is skillful at communicating with people, understanding their perspective, and relaying that to a client, then this could be a great business idea for you. You would help clients engage with their customers to understand their needs better, which helps both your client and their customer get what they want. If you're good at it, this can be a great business opportunity.

◻ Children Products

Schools have been closed during the pandemic and children stayed at home. Their parents had to quickly discover how to entertain and educate them. Children's books and online education recorded an enormous boom and many became bestsellers overnight, literally. After the restrictions are lifted and life returns to "normal" these sales will drop. However, if the restrictions last longer, people get used to them and may find that these forms of education and entertainment have a better influence on children than TV or the internet, and may keep higher demand for these products. I mentioned just two children's products but there are many more if you look around with open eyes. Just remember that children are not your target customers, but their parents are. When you choose your products, design them to their parents' needs, what they think is good for their children.

These ideas are some of the more promising online business ideas, but there are other ways to profit from online businesses. For example, it is also possible to buy an existing, developed-online business if you have the appropriate funds. In this scenario, you would then continue building customer share and business profits.

You can buy or build a business and sell it in the future. Sales price is estimated from future years' profits. It's even possible to earn much more if you are approached by a company looking to build a dominant share of that particular market. In a sense, it's like those realtors who buy a house, fix it up, and then sell it for a profit. There are other ideas similar to this one too, and it some-times pays to think outside the box.

Whatever kind of online business you may choose, the key to succeed is to focus on customer needs and find innovative and efficient ways to serve those needs. If you can do that, you can build an enduring online business that will enable you to live your dreams. There are a few pitfalls to avoid, which will be addressed in the next chapter.

Chapter Summary

In this chapter, we went through numerous examples of promising online business opportunities in the current climate. Specifically, we covered the following topics:

- Entrepreneurial winners.
- Online businesses that involve innovative technology.
- Online businesses that involve marketing strategies.
- Entrepreneurial online business ideas.
- Business build-up, renovation, and resale.

In the next chapter, we'll go over the pitfalls to avoid with online entrepreneurship.

---

[15] https://www.entrepreneur.com/article/299734

[16] https://www.emarketer.com/newsroom/index.php/us-digital-ad-spending-will-surpass-traditional-in-2019/

Chapter TEN

ONLINE ENTREPRENEURSHIP– WHAT TO LOOK OUT FOR

IF you plan to take the leap into the online business world, you will want to do everything you can to ensure it will be successful. The internet has incredible potential, and you have an opportunity right now to jump into this profitable realm. Research shows that approximately 70% of Americans shop online, and the US e-commerce revenue in 2019 was more than $600 billion[17] (Digital Commerce 360, 2020). However, online business opportunities come with their own set of unique challenges, and you could encounter some devastating pitfalls if you don't know what to watch out for. Let's take a look at the pitfalls you'll want to avoid.

Taking Too Long to Launch

As the saying goes, timing is everything, and nowhere is that more true than when you go to launch a business. If you spend too much time researching your business or waiting for the perfect execution, you can miss your launch window. Don't let what's perfect be the enemy of the good. If you do, it's possible a competitor will beat you to the punch. Additionally, you shouldn't let yourself fall into the trap of analysis paralysis—avoid overthinking and worrying too much about being perfect. Make it good and get it out there.

Starting a Business You're Not Passionate About

If you want to start your own business, there's one thing for certain—you will spend a lot of time thinking about it and a lot of time working on it, so you'd better like it. You will have to be dedicated to sticking with it, even when the profits aren't that high. In fact, that will be when you have to stay the most invested. There will be many obstacles you might face; things like more competition than you had anticipated, and, if you aren't enthusiastic about getting up every day to make this business work, it won't. It's that simple. Your lack of enthusiasm will show in every aspect of your business, and your customers and employees will all be able to pick up on it. Therefore, whatever business you choose to start, make sure you're passionate about it.

Underestimating the Time It Will Take to Make Profit

Many businesses won't make a profit in their first year, and you have to be realistic about the work it will take to make the profit you're hoping for. You have to put in as much work for an online business as you would a brick and mortar business. It takes a lot of time, energy, and planning, and you shouldn't make the mistake of thinking it will be quick and easy. You can start to earn money relatively quickly, but that is not the same thing as making a profit. Set realistic goals and manage your expectations. You'll get there, but it will take some time.

Failing to Prepare

While it can be fast and relatively easy to start an online business, you would still have to prepare. That means doing your homework by researching your niche, identifying your clients, choosing a business model, setting your prices, preparing your marketing strategy, and personally defining success. There are many aspects of your business that will evolve over time; however, if you don't start out with a plan, you will likely never see your launch date, let alone succeed.

Fixing Something That Isn't Broken

A common reason many online businesses fail is that they are offering a product or service that doesn't solve any significant problem for their clients. Remember that a problem you identify also has to be a problem that your potential customers have identified. If they don't think it's a problem, they won't buy your solution. In addition, if you see that has happened and don't pivot your online business in a different direction, you can lose it altogether. Make sure your goal is always to address the customers' needs. If you don't do that, you won't have customers.

Dismissing Negative Feedback

It can be easy—and certainly more gratifying—to listen to your fans and ignore your critics, but this is a mistake that will completely undermine your business. You need to listen to the negative reviews, so you can understand your customers better, tweak your product as necessary, and develop top-notch customer service. Consumers will also be paying quite a bit of attention to those negative reviews, so you need to as well. Let the negative feedback guide you to improve your business, and solicit feedback regularly to keep track of customer satisfaction.

Not Being Unique Enough

You have to find a way to distinguish yourself from the competition. If too many businesses are doing the same thing, then there are too many businesses in that niche. To really get traction in your area, you have to be different and offer something that the other guy isn't. It could be a unique product, but it could also be a unique delivery method, faster delivery, or perks that others aren't offering. Ask yourself: what can I offer that my competitors can't, or how can I be different in your niche? You have to make it clear to your target audience why they should choose you over the competition.

Failing to Define Your Target Audience

You must identify who your ideal customers are and tailor your marketing efforts toward them. Understand that you simply will be unable to fill the needs of every consumer, and the object is to figure out who can use your online business best and how you can meet their needs. That will allow you to market directly to your ideal customers, generating the highest revenue. You can also compete better against larger companies by targeting a niche audience. You will want to include your target audience in your business plan, particularly if you're seeking investors.

Undervaluing What You're Selling

Whether you're selling a product or service, you have to determine an appropriate price that will enable you to make a profit. It can be tempting to undervalue what you're selling to beat out the competition; however, similar to how it is with freelance work, the emphasis has to be on quality rather than price. Customers will pay for quality, and they will come back for more when they know you can produce that high quality.

Skimping on Early Hires

In the effort to quickly fill positions, it's easy to rush the hiring process. That can lead, however, to a mismatch of skills and business needs, bad personality fit with the company culture, and/or lack of commitment to the company's mission. Therefore, before you hire someone to represent your business with clients, be sure you choose the one with the skills you value and the drive to help make your business a success. Remember—they will be making the first impressions with your clients, thus, if that goes badly, it will leave a mark.

There are certainly other pitfalls to look out for, but these are some of the most common ones that cause online businesses to fail. If you can avoid these and surround yourself with people who will give you constructive advice for navigating online business, you will then give yourself a better chance of succeeding.

Chapter Summary

In this chapter, we discussed several common pitfalls that you should avoid to have a better chance of succeeding with your online business. Specifically, we went over the following potential pitfalls:

- Failure to prepare and plan properly.
- Offering a product people aren't buying.
- Ignoring customer feedback and/or not defining your ideal client.
- Undervaluing your product and/or not being unique enough in your business.
- Skimping on hires and underestimating the time you need to make a profit.

[17] https://www.digitalcommerce360.com/article/us-ecommerce-sales/

FINAL WORDS

WE live in uncertain times, but there is still a way you can take more control over your livelihood that doesn't have to be an impetuous response to a crisis. You can take some time to consider whether online or remote work may be right for you, and there are solutions that will work for you, regardless of your level of experience or technological acumen. The coronavirus crisis may be what pushed you into considering this kind of change in your life, but the solution doesn't have to be temporary. You can get into freelance work or open your own online business, and you can decide then, after this pandemic, whether you want to continue with that lifestyle too.

If you ever thought about living life on your own terms, doing something you're passionate about, and taking control of your own destiny, now is your chance to make that a reality. Freelance work is a growing trend, and online businesses are burgeoning, thus you have an opportunity to change your life for the better. The impetus for change may have been a crisis, but you can turn it into an opportunity to change your life fundamentally and take control of your future.

Experts predict that the coronavirus pandemic will permanently change the workforce in at least three ways[18] (Stahl, 2020):

- *More telecommuting*—the remote workforce has already grown 91% over the last decade, and not only with the reality of the coronavirus contagion, but the realization that this could happen again. Therefore, remote work will only become more commonplace. This situation creates enormous opportunities for freelance work and online businesses.

- *Rise in unlimited sick days*—with people being concerned about exposing coworkers to possible contagions, there is likely to be an increase in sick days as more people understand the importance of staying home when they don't feel well. This point would also highlight one of the benefits of online work—you will be less likely to catch anything, and you won't be spreading anything to others either.

◻ *Increased reliance on tech over travel*—with businesses being forced to use video conferencing rather than commuting, it's likely that technology will see significant bottom-line advantages that will result in permanent changes. This fact thus opens up a whole slew of opportunities for innovative online and freelance businesses. Artificial intelligence solutions and the online businesses to market them can help businesses of every kind make that transition. Telecommunication solutions offer a real alternative to travel, and virtual reality tools can provide employees with training rather than sending them to retreats.

There may be many more changes that will result from this crisis, but just these three represent tremendous opportunities for getting into the online workforce. We may not have asked for this situation, but you can take advantage of it. With the techniques and tips I've given you in this book, you now have the information you need to get started today on a new lifestyle—one in which you can take charge of your own future. In addition, one where you can create the kind of life you've only seen in your dreams. Seize the day, and you can emerge from this crisis with a new life where you call the shots, have more time to spend with your family, and can take time to relax whenever you want. It's up to you now. You can do it, and you are good enough to make it happen. Now, you have the knowledge you need to succeed!

Today is a great day to create your future!

---

[18] https://www.forbes.com/sites/ashleystahl/2020/03/12/3-ways-coronavirus-may-impact-the-future-of-the-workforce/#951e23e1cef5

References

Adams, R. L. *(2019, March 7)*. **7 Online Business Ideas That Could Make You Rich.** *Retrieved March 27, 2020, from https://www.entrepreneur.com/article/299734*

Beat, T. *(2019, October 13)*. **10 Mistakes to Avoid When Starting an Online Business.** *Retrieved March 29, 2020, from https://infobeat.com/10-mistakes-to-avoid-when-starting-an-online-business/*

Braccio-Hering, B. *(2020, February 13)*. **Remote Work Statistics: Shifting Norms and Expectations.** *Retrieved March 20, 2020, from https://www.flexjobs.com/blog/post/remote-work-statistics/*

Bradberry, T. *(2015, January 20)*. **Multitasking Damages Your Brain And Career, New Studies Suggest.** *Retrieved March 20, 2020, from https://www.forbes.com/sites/travisbradberry/2014/10/08/multitasking-damages-your-brain-and-career-new-studies-suggest/#1a0bb6ce56ee*

Braverman Rega, S. B. B. *(2019, December 14)*. **The highest-paying freelance jobs of 2020 where you can earn $90,000 or more.** *Retrieved from https://www.cnbc.com/2019/12/14/highest-paying-freelance-jobs-of-2020-where-you-earn-90000-or-more.html*

C. *(2019, June 18)*. **Start-up Mistakes to Avoid When Starting an Online Business.** *Retrieved March 29, 2020, from https://codersera.com/blog/start-up-mistakes-to-avoid-when-starting-an-online-business/*

Cohen, E. S. M. C. *(2020, March 19)*. **Asymptomatic people without coronavirus symptoms might be driving the spread more than we realized.** *Retrieved March 19, 2020, from https://edition.cnn.com/2020/03/14/health/coronavirus-asymptomatic-spread/index.html*

Contributor, G. *(2017, September 11)*. **5 things to consider before becoming a freelancer.** *Retrieved March 20, 2020, from https://www.thejobnetwork.com/5-things-to-consider-before-becoming-a-freelancer/*

Corcione, D. *(2017, August 2)*. **Freelancing 101: What Every Potential Freelancer Should Know.** *Retrieved March 20, 2020, from https://www.businessnewsdaily.com/5242-freelancer-tips.html*

Darlington, N. *(2020, February 2)*. **Freelancer vs. Contractor vs. Employee: What Are You Being Hired As | FreshBooks Blog.** *Retrieved March 20, 2020, from https://www.freshbooks.com/blog/are-you-being-hired-as-an-employee-or-freelancer*

DesMarais, C. *(2020, February 6)*. **Get More Done: 18 Tips for Telecommuters.** *Retrieved March 20, 2020, from https://www.inc.com/christina-desmarais/get-more-done-18-tips-for-telecommuters.html*

Devaney, E. *(n.d.)*. **How to Work From Home: 20 Tips From People Who Do It Successfully.** *Retrieved March 20, 2020, from https://blog.hubspot.com/marketing/productivity-tips-working-from-home*

Digital Commerce 360. *(2020, March 9)*. **US ecommerce sales grow 14.9% in 2019.** *Retrieved March 28, 2020, from https://www.digitalcommerce360.com/article/us-ecommerce-sales/*

Dishman, L. *(2020, March 11)*. **8 strategies to set up remote work during the coronavirus outbreak.** *Retrieved March 20, 2020, from https://www.fastcompany.com/90475330/8-strategies-to-set-up-remote-work-during-the-coronavirus-outbreak*

Ducharme, J. *(2020, March 9)*. **The WHO Estimated COVID-19 Mortality at 3.4%. That Doesn't Tell the Whole Story.** *Retrieved March 19, 2020, from https://time.com/5798168/coronavirus-mortality-rate/*

Duermyer, R. *(2019, August 9)*. **Becoming an At-Home Freelancer.** *Retrieved March 20, 2020, from https://www.thebalancesmb.com/how-to-become-a-freelancer-1794507*

Elorus Team. *(2019, July 17)*. **Choosing a Pricing Model that Fits your Freelance Business.** *Retrieved March 24, 2020, from https://www.elorus.com/blog/choosing-a-pricing-model-that-fits-your-freelance-business/*

eMarketer. *(2019, February 20).* » US Digital Ad Spending Will Surpass Traditional in 2019 eMarketer Newsroom. *Retrieved March 28, 2020, from https://www.emarketer.com/newsroom/index. php/us-digital-ad-spending-will-surpass-traditional-in-2019/*

Emerson, M. *(2017, January 9).* **17 Steps to Launching a Freelance Business.** *Retrieved March 24, 2020, from https://succeedasyourownboss.com/17-steps-launching-freelance-business/*

F., I. *(2020a, January 2).* **18 Best Freelance Websites to Find Work in 2020.** *Retrieved March 24, 2020, from https://www.hostinger.com/tutorials/best-freelance-websites*

F., I. *(2020b, January 2).* **18 Best Freelance Websites to Find Work in 2020.** *Retrieved March 25, 2020, from https://www.hostinger.com/tutorials/best-freelance-websites*

Farrer, L. *(2020, March 17).* **Remote Work Advocates Warn Companies About COVID-19 Work-From-Home Strategies.** *Retrieved March 20, 2020, from https://www.forbes.com/sites/ laurelfarrer/2020/03/05/ironically-remote-work-advocates-warn-companies-about-covid-19-work-from-home-strategies/#f82c76b20515*

Francia, L. *(2014, April 23).* **8 Common Freelancing Mistakes You Can Avoid.** *Retrieved March 26, 2020, from https://www.lifehack.org/articles/work/8-common-freelancing-mistakes-you-can-avoid.html*

Gillivan, C. *(2020a, March 9).* **68 Best Freelance Job Sites for Getting Clients in 2020.** *Retrieved March 24, 2020, from https://millo.co/freelance-job-sites*

Gillivan, C. *(2020b, March 9).* **68 Best Freelance Job Sites for Getting Clients in 2020.** *Retrieved March 25, 2020, from https://millo.co/freelance-job-sites*

Guidant Financial. *(2019, November 7).* **10 Tax Advantages of C Corporations.** *Retrieved March 24, 2020, from https://www.guidantfinancial.com/blog/10-tax-benefits-of-c-corporations/*

Hamm, T. *(2018, October 31).* **Seven Strategies for Working from Home from an Experienced Telecommuter.** *Retrieved March 20, 2020, from https://www.thesimpledollar.com/make-money/seven-strategies-for-working-from-home-from-an-experienced-telecommuter/*

Haskins, J. E. *(2019, June 20).* **How to Start an Online Business in 8 Steps.** *Retrieved March 28, 2020, from https://www.legalzoom.com/articles/how-to-start-an-online-business-in-8-steps*

Howington, J. *(2019, October 24).* **The 20 Most Popular Work-from-Home Job Titles.** *Retrieved March 20, 2020, from https://www.flexjobs.com/blog/post/20-most-common-work-from-home-job-titles-v2/*

K., K. *(2015, October 9).* **How to Set Up an Online Business - Complete Beginner's Guide.** *Retrieved March 28, 2020, from http://newinternetorder.com/how-to-set-up-an-online-business/*

Kachan, D. *(2019, May 16).* **Psychology in Web Design: Exploring Hidden Influences on Users' Decision-Making.** *Retrieved March 27, 2020, from https://www.business2community.com/web-design/psychology-in-web-design-exploring-hidden-influences-on-users-decision-making-02200931*

LegalNature. *(n.d.).* **17 Mistakes To Avoid When Starting An Online Business | LegalNature.** *Retrieved March 29, 2020, from https://www.legalnature.com/guides/17-mistakes-to-avoid-when-starting-an-online-business*

Levine, L. *(2019, October 29).* **4 Types of Freelance Clients You Should Avoid at All Costs.** *Retrieved March 26, 2020, from https://www.themuse.com/advice/4-types-of-freelance-clients-you-should-avoid-at-all-costs*

Limited, S. H. K. *(2019, September 30).* **15 Best Ecommerce Business Ideas to Start in 2020.** *Retrieved March 28, 2020, from https://medium.com/@startupr/15-best-ecommerce-business-ideas-to-start-in-2020-daa28febf1d0*

Maguire, A. (*2019, October 9*). **Top 6 Problems Freelancers Face (and What to Do About Them).** *Retrieved March 26, 2020, from https://www.businessknowhow.com/startup/top-freelancing-problems.htm*

Miles. (*2020, March 27*). **Top 10 Online Business Ideas in 2020 – How to Make 10k a Month.** *Retrieved March 27, 2020, from https://www.milesbeckler.com/best-online-business-ideas/*

Moon, A. (*2019, November 4*). **7 Steps to Starting a Small Business Online.** *Retrieved March 28, 2020, from https://www.entrepreneur.com/article/175242*

Moraes, M. (*2020, January 6*). **82 Best Business Ideas For Newbie Entrepreneurs [2020...** *Retrieved March 27, 2020, from https://digital.com/blog/best-business-ideas/*

Nastor, J. (*2019, December 12*). **6 Online Business Models (and How to Get Customers).** *Retrieved March 28, 2020, from https://hacktheentrepreneur.com/online-business-models/*

Patterson, M. (*2014, June 11*). **How to Be Productive and Stay Sane Working at Home: 7 Success Strategies.** *Retrieved March 20, 2020, from https://www.lifehack.org/articles/work/how-productive-and-stay-sane-working-home-7-success-strategies.html*

PCMag. (*2020, March 20*). **20 Tips for Working From Home.** *Retrieved March 20, 2020, from https://www.pcmag.com/news/get-organized-20-tips-for-working-from-home*

Pinola, M. (*2016, February 25*). **Freelancer or Employee: Your Best Arguments.** *Retrieved March 20, 2020, from https://lifehacker.com/freelancer-or-employee-your-best-arguments-1761233384*

Pozin, I. (*2020, February 6*). **5 Things to Consider If You Think Freelancing Is in Your Future.** *Retrieved March 20, 2020, from https://www.inc.com/ilya-pozin/5-things-to-consider-before-taking-plunge-into-freelancing.html*

Prakash, J. P. D. (*2017, December 8*). **How to Set Up a Business Entity as a Freelancer.** *Retrieved March 24, 2020, from https://www.fundera.com/blog/how-to-set-up-a-business-entity-as-a-freelancer*

Robinson, R. (*2020a, February 27*). **78 Best Freelance Jobs Websites to Get Remote Freelance Work (Fast) in 2020.** *Retrieved March 24, 2020, from https://www.ryrob.com/freelance-jobs/*

Robinson, R. (*2020b, February 27*). **78 Best Freelance Jobs Websites to Get Remote Freelance Work (Fast) in 2020.** *Retrieved March 25, 2020, from https://www.ryrob.com/freelance-jobs/#writing*

Robinson, R. (*2020c, February 28*). **10 Steps How to Start a Freelancing Business While Working Full-Time in 2020 (and Why You Should).** *Retrieved March 24, 2020, from https://www.ryrob.com/why-freelance-while-working-full-time-and-how-to-do-it/*

Robinson, R. (*2020d, March 13*). **Infographic: Are You Charging the Right Hourly Rate as a Freelancer?** *Retrieved March 24, 2020, from https://www.ryrob.com/infographic-freelance-hourly-rate-setting-your-price/*

Schäferhoff, N. (*2019, December 21*). **Online Business Ideas.** *Retrieved March 27, 2020, from https://websitesetup.org/online-business-ideas/*

Staff, T. S. D. (*2020, January 28*). **The Ultimate Freelancer's Guide: Everything You Need to Know About Getting Jobs, Getting Paid and Getting Ahead.** *Retrieved March 20, 2020, from https://www.thesimpledollar.com/financial-wellness/ultimate-freelancers-guide/*

Stahl, A. (*2020, March 12*). **3 Ways The Coronavirus Outbreak May Change The Workforce.** *Retrieved March 29, 2020, from https://www.forbes.com/sites/ashleystahl/2020/03/12/3-ways-coronavirus-may-impact-the-future-of-the-workforce/#951e23e1cef5*

Stanford News. (*2009, August 24*). **Media multitaskers pay mental price, Stanford study shows.** *Retrieved March 20, 2020, from https://news.stanford.edu/news/2009/august24/multitask-research-study-082409.html*

Stanford University. *(2018, October 25)*. Heavy multitaskers have reduced memory. *Retrieved March 20, 2020, from https://news.stanford.edu/2018/10/25/decade-data-reveals-heavy-multitaskers-reduced-memory-psychologist-says/*

Stolzoff, S. *(2018, November 2)*. The number of freelance workers in the United States is climbing. *Retrieved March 21, 2020, from https://qz.com/work/1441108/the-us-now-has-more-than-56-7-million-freelance-workers-and-they-vote/*

Sun, C. *(2016, March 7)*. 10 Mistakes to Avoid When Starting an Online Business. *Retrieved March 29, 2020, from https://www.entrepreneur.com/article/250698*

Truex, L. *(2018, December 17)*. How to Start a Resume Writing Service Pros, Cons, and Steps to Helping Others Land a Job. *Retrieved March 28, 2020, from https://www.thebalancesmb.com/how-to-start-a-resume-writing-service-3957645*

Twago, T. *(2016, February 25)*. 7 mistakes freelancers should avoid. *Retrieved March 26, 2020, from https://www.twago.com/blog/7-mistakes-freelancers-should-avoid-the-etiquette-guide-for-freelancers/*

Uncapher, M. R., & Wagner, A. D. *(2018)*. Minds and brains of media multitaskers: Current findings and future directions. *Proceedings of the National Academy of Sciences, 115(40), 9889–9896. https://doi.org/10.1073/pnas.1611612115*

Upwork. *(2019a)*. Freelancing in America: 2019 Survey - Upwork. *Retrieved March 24, 2020, from https://www.upwork.com/i/freelancing-in-america/*

Upwork. *(2019b, November 15)*. Sixth annual "Freelancing in America" study finds that more people than ever see freelancing as a long-term career path. *Retrieved March 25, 2020, from https://www.upwork.com/press/2019/10/03/freelancing-in-america-2019/*

Upwork and Freelancers Union. *(2017, October 29)*. Freelancers predicted to become the U.S. workforce majority within a decade, with nearly 50% of millennial workers already freelancing, annual "Freelancing in America" study finds. Retrieved March 20, 2020, *from https://www.upwork.com/press/2017/10/17/freelancing-in-america-2017/*

U.S. Bureau of Labor Statistics. *(2019, September 4)*. Technical Writers : Occupational Outlook Handbook: : U.S. Bureau of Labor Statistics. Retrieved March 28, 2020, *from https://www.bls.gov/ooh/media-and-communication/technical-writers.htm*

van Doremalen, N., Bushmaker, T., Morris, D. H., Holbrook, M. G., Gamble, A., Williamson, B. N., ... Munster, V. J. *(2020)*. Aerosol and Surface Stability of SARS-CoV-2 as Compared with SARS-CoV-1. New England Journal of Medicine. *https://doi.org/10.1056/nejmc2004973*

wikiHow. *(2020, February 6)*. How to Start an Affiliate Marketing Business. *Retrieved March 28, 2020, from https://www.wikihow.com/Start-an-Affiliate-Marketing-Business*

WorldOmeter. *(2020, March 19)*. Coronavirus Update (Live): 244,364 Cases and 10,007 Deaths from COVID-19 Virus Outbreak - Worldometer. Retrieved March 19, 2020, *from https://www.worldometers.info/coronavirus/*

WP Shastra. *(2020a, March 21)*. 10 Best Freelance Websites in the World | 2020. *Retrieved from https://wpshastra.com/best-freelance-websites/*

WP Shastra. *(2020b, March 21)*. 10 Best Freelance Websites in the World | 2020. Retrieved March 25, 2020, *from https://wpshastra.com/best-freelance-websites/*

Writing, F. *(2018, April 26)*. Avoid These 10 Common Freelancing Traps to Run a More Successful Writing Business. *Retrieved March 26, 2020, from https://www.freelancewriting.com/feature-articles/common-freelancing-traps/*

Zetlin, M. *(2020, February 6)*. For the Most Productive Workday, Science Says Make Sure to Do This. *Retrieved March 20, 2020, from https://www.inc.com/minda-zetlin/productivity-workday-52-minutes-work-17-minutes-break-travis-bradberry-pomodoro-technique.html*

SAVE MONEY
AND
SPEND
WISELY

DURING AND AFTER
THE ECONOMIC CRISIS

Personal Finance Tips for Managing Money and Budgeting Wisely in Difficult Times

DANA WISE

SAVE MONEY AND SPEND WISELY

INTRODUCTION

DO you find the current economic upheaval scary? Not sure what to do about it? Well, you're not alone! It's not clear what the ultimate impact will be, but despite the uncertainty, there are still many things that you can do personally to manage your money wisely during this time.

As of now (March 2020), we don't know how long the current restrictions will last, and like plenty of others, you may not have any income coming in. Unfortunately, what we do know is that bills will continue despite that lack of income! There may be some relief coming in from different institutions, but for the most part, bills must be paid on the savings we already have.

That doesn't mean all is lost, however. You can decide to spend wisely now and consider your purchases carefully before you buy them. There are some immediate solutions you can put into place, along with medium and long-term steps you can take to shore up your financial situation.

Human brains prefer certainty, which is partly why the current atmosphere feels so frightening with all the unknowns in the air. Once you develop a plan for your finances, however, you'll find that life no longer seems so uncertain. Managing your money means that you are taking control of your funds, and our brains like that feeling of control! I like it as well as you!

Once you've started saving money using the practical tips provided within this book, you will find saving money will be much easier for you. Even if you found it difficult before, and especially if you had never really paid attention to your personal finances, you will discover why it's important for developing a mastery of your money.

Your money is a tool—nothing more. It doesn't define who you are as a person, and it shouldn't run your life. Learning how to use this tool properly will not only help you get through this economic upheaval relatively unscathed. In doing so, you will also greatly empower yourself.

Many people avoid thinking about their money or try to manage it proactively because they don't like numbers or math. Again, good news! The biggest factor to successful money management is actually your mindset, and you will learn how to think about your finances correctly and avoid bad decisions. That is really the key to personal finance.

In this book, I will be showing you how to achieve that successful money mindset and discussing the importance of goals. It can sometimes be challenging to forego your current spending habits, but it will be much easier once you have something tangible to save for. In some ways, the current coronavirus epidemic may actually help you spend less money. With bars, restaurants, and movie theaters shut down for an unknown period of time, you will have fewer places to spend money unthinkingly.

One essential tip for managing your money wisely is to know exactly how you're spending money. Many people, after monthly payments for rent, utilities, and other fixed costs, don't really know how they should spend the rest of their income. You will learn how to track your spending and figure out where all that money went. We will also be discussing the importance of setting aside an emergency fund, even if you can't manage to save an entire three months' worth of expenses at the moment.

Recognizing what you value will also be incredibly helpful because such will allow you to focus your spending on that and cut back on other expenses. When you don't spend on things you don't really care about, you won't feel as deprived, thus actually allowing you to stick to your spending plan.

Another critical factor in personal finance is recognizing that done is better than perfect. You can't save the maximum for your retirement contribution? That's OK, you can save a little, which is better than none. Can't cut out all your sports spending? That's OK, you can cut back on the things that you don't necessarily need or want right now. 151

With the tips in this book, you will learn how to manage your spending once this crisis has passed. And it will, as they always do. You'll come out of the pandemic with solid knowledge about personal finance that you will be able to use to your advantage for the rest of your life. You will understand the difference between wants and needs and learn how to budget for both.

Did you know that understanding a topic gives you power over it? Right now, you may be feeling a bit powerless and thinking that you can do hardly anything in terms of your money. Get ready to change that because reading this book will help you learn how to take action.

In addition to exploring your own goals, we will be going over some practical tips for managing your funds. The chapters about spending are divided into quick actions you can take right now, medium-term suggestions that you can use in the next few months, and long-term advice that may take you a bit more time and effort to add into your daily routines. Toward the end is when we will be discussing how you can take all this knowledge into the future and stay motivated, even when you don't have a financial crisis to spur you on.

I will show you the positive future consequences of the decisions you make today, and you will see the many compounding benefits to receive just from choosing one right decision. The benefits of good decision-making go well beyond saving money—they will also improve other areas of your life, including your mental and physical health and well-being.

It is easy for anyone to implement the tips and ideas from this book into their life, and you don't need to be a finance or math whiz to do them. You probably don't even need a calculator! You just need to know what's important to you. It's not about what other people are spending or even how they are dealing with their money during the crisis; it's about you and your family being smart about it.

Mindless spending happens quite often in a consumerist society, which is what we are living in right now. By the end of this book, you will cease to be another mindless consumer; instead, you will be a savvy spender, and you will be able to maximize your budget for your specific situation.

Right now, you may be wondering—what qualifies me to give you all this advice? How credible am I?

I have been in the financial industry for years and have helped people just like you to take control of their money. I was in finance when we didn't have easy apps to help us balance out the portfolio, track spending, or even round up our spending to invest the difference. Now, it's incredibly easy for people to track their spending without having to write down every expense in a notebook or spreadsheet!

I have spent a lot of time coaching people through their spending plans. Including how to identify the low-hanging fruit on their spending that they can cut back easily without feeling deprived. And, figuring out what is important to them so they can spend appropriately. Many think that people with lots of money know what to do with it, and I can tell you for a fact that that is not true! I have assisted people who have a lot of money, along with those who don't have a lot of money.

Most people I have worked with really didn't know how to handle their finances, no matter their bank balance or how educated they were in finance. It's not a topic taught often in most schools, nor will you really find college courses about it either. However, as a former financial planner, I think everyone should understand the basics of finance!

You may not know this, and most people won't tell you because they don't want you thinking critically about your money, but mindless purchasing costs much more than you would think. Suppose you earned $10; $2 went to taxes, and maybe you saved

$1 for retirement. However, you spent the rest of it. Do you know where that $7 went?

Don't worry—I have ideas for you to save several dollars from each $10 earned without feeling deprived. The quicker you can take control, the better. Doing so will not just help with your finances, but your mental health as well.

Lately, I've seen a lot of people panicking about their money during this time of upheaval. No judgment because it's perfectly understandable! The pandemic response kicked off a recession, which has historically made even the most shrewd investors nervous about their money. I've been through recessions, including the Great Recession of 2008-2009, and helped guide people through it. Our country has been through pandemics before, and it undoubtedly will again.

But you must act now! The longer you wait to learn about and implement these tips, the harder it will be to take action. If you're overspending now on things that don't matter to you, you are literally draining your money faster than you need to. The sooner you can halt the mindless spending and reduce what you spend on "wants," the stronger your finances will be.

The actions I recommend will benefit you both in the short term and long term while making your brain happy. By reading this book, you will learn new actions that you can take right away, so don't hesitate when you have the chance now to triumph over current circumstances.

Today is a great day to create your future, so let's get started!

Chapter **ONE**

KNOW THYSELF: SPENDING AND GOALS

THIS chapter will focus on creating the right framework for implementing the steps found in the following chapters. Because we will be going over some relevant information for the next sections in this book, it would be a terrible idea to skip this all-important first chapter! If you don't learn why you should cut back on certain items and don't figure out an overall goal to look toward, you will have a lot of difficulty in sticking to your plan.

Have you ever tried to master your money before but ended up splurging, thus depleting your savings? It's pretty common, and it means that you probably didn't know what you really wanted to spend money on, or specifically why you wanted to reduce your spending; you didn't have a concrete goal to work toward.

Not running out of money during the coronavirus crisis may seem like a pretty good reason to avoid spending money, and it absolutely is! There are closures occurring across entertainment, among other businesses. However, if that's your only reason to stop splurging, such a thought process won't help your future behavior once the current crisis is over. You will need another reason that's not influenced by short-term events.

Mindset

We mentioned in the introduction that our brains prefer certainty and action, which are two principal cognitive biases that all humans evolved to have, among plenty of others. Most other biases, however, were adaptations that helped us when we were early humans living on the savannah and needed to worry about where our next meal would be coming from, and whether we ourselves were to become a tiger's next meal!

Those older biases don't necessarily work now in the modern world, however. We may still have our wild savannah-adapted brains in a decidedly non-savannah world, though human beings in developed nations don't really have to worry about where their next meal is coming from. We don't even have to go get it; we can have the next meal delivered to our doorstep with nothing more than a bit of typing, and we are not being stalked by tigers.

However—and especially during a recession and this Coronavirus crisis—we do worry about being capitalism's next meal because that is where the money to pay our bills and keep the lights on and a roof over our heads comes from. Thinking that we can't earn any money because our workplace shut down due to the coronavirus or possibly a recession is a scary thought.

Being frightened is located mainly in the part of our brains that we inherited from our reptilian ancestors, and you may have heard it called **reptilian** or **lizard brain** as a result. It is 157 where we have our *fight-or-flight* reaction, and is also known as the **amygdala**.

The rational part of our brain evolved later. It loves resources and information and works slowly, at least compared to the amygdala. This part of the brain is in the **frontal lobe**, and it helps you evaluate the advantages and disadvantages between certain options you may be considering at any time.

When the body's stress response is activated, your heart beats faster and you may start breathing hard. The stress hormone cortisol is released, and the brain essentially takes the rational portion offline. There's no time for weighing the pros and cons of running away from a tiger because, if you did that, you would probably be eaten. The brain wants to survive, so it activates the fight-or-flight reaction when threatened. However, when the amygdala is in charge, the rational section of the brain won't function well enough to put together an appropriate response.

Why does this matter? Well, our brains can't tell the difference between the fear of being eaten by a tiger and the fear of running out of money. Fear is fear, so the brain releases cortisol, starts to prepare the body to run away from the tiger, taking down those rational functions in the process. This process means that, when you're stressed, panicked, or afraid in terms of current events, you literally cannot think straight.

This fear is completely natural. We're facing an uncertain world, so it would make sense that you are feeling fearful, anxious, and as if you lack control. However, when it comes to making good financial decisions and managing your money, you will need your rational brain in a completely functional state. In some circumstances, that will mean that you work around your fears. There are some tricks you can use to bring your rational thought back online once stressed but need to make decisions.

o The serenity statement

"...grant me the serenity to accept the things I cannot change, the courage to change the things I can, and the wisdom to know the difference." —Reinhold Niebuhr

There are a lot of things in the modern world that we simply have no control over, and this obviously includes certain viruses, including the novel coronavirus! What government leaders will say and do in response to a crisis is not something an individual citizen has control over—the only thing we can do is vote out politicians who don't do their jobs properly.

Stock market returns are beyond our control, at least in the short term. We know that, on average, the stock market returns 8-10% over a long period. However, what it will do in the short term is anyone's guess.

We don't know which businesses will close permanently or what life will look like once the current crisis is over. There is also uncertainty about what exactly our "new normal" will look like. That normal could be similar to life before the coronavirus, but we won't really know until then.

Worrying about these things is completely futile because there's nothing we can do about them. Thinking too much about these topics will cause our amygdala to rule us, which means we'll start making terrible decisions.

Cortisol and the related stress response is fine for us in short bursts, like it was with our ancestors. However, when it's released almost constantly, as it is for some people, it causes long-term damage to your body and shortens your life.

Instead, consider what you can change. You have a vote, so use it when election day rolls around. Don't just consider this for the big national elections, but local ones too. You decide how much you want to save and what you want to spend, unless 159 you're at or below the poverty line. You know what your skills are, and you should learn how to leverage them.

Wisdom comes when you figure out what you have control over and what you can change. It should be pretty obvious that no single individual has any control over the stock market with the billions of trades being executed regularly.

You have no control over what anyone else does. To a certain extent, you even lack control over your own thoughts and emotions! Your brain's job is to generate thoughts, and so it does, but not all of these thoughts are helpful, useful, or relevant. You'll also experience certain feelings, which just happen. Let them happen, because you will get in trouble by trying to repress them!

However, what you can command is your response to these thoughts and feelings. You don't have to react to them right away, if at all. The thoughts that don't serve you can be let go, released onto a leaf in a mental stream flowing away from you, or visualized as a cloud that appears and then disappears.

You may be feeling stressed or scared, which is perfectly fine. However, it's not usually fine to take action based on those emotions before you've thought them through.

o Take control where you can

Remember that human brains like action and being in control! Therefore, don't spend your valuable time worrying about something that you have no personal influence over. Instead, spend it thinking about the actions you can take to make positive changes.

Make a plan that will outline how you will be spending your money. Find a place where you can cut back your spending and then just do it. When you do pleasurable things, like taking action, your brain will release a little bit of **dopamine**, which is known as the "feel-good" neurotransmitter. Therefore, when you take that action, you'll feel good.

When you see the results of your actions, you will feel like you're back in control, which will then hit you with another dose of dopamine! Tracking your spending, creating financial goals, and shifting money to better places are all situations that give you pleasure and will help you in the long term.

o Take deep breaths and do math

I know, *I know* I said there wouldn't be any math! However, math is a great way to bring your rational functions back after your stress response takes over.

Deep breathing is another way to slow down your stress. When you're afraid and getting ready to run away from that tiger, your breathing speeds up because your body needs some quick hits of oxygen for either flight or fight. By slowing your breathing down deliberately, you signal the lack of threat to your amygdala[1] (Goleman, 2005). Your brain, realizing the tiger's gone, will stop its stress response, which allows rational function to take over again. Doing math also brings your "thinking" brain back to the forefront. It doesn't necessarily have to be complicated math; there's no need for calculus unless you really want it.

Are you making lists of expenses and amounts you want to cut back on, adding up columns of spending, and comparing last month's spending to this month's?

Human brains are puzzle and problem solvers. If you give your brain a math problem, it will naturally want to solve it. Since the amygdala is quite hopeless when it comes to numbers, rational function will have to start working again to solve the problem.

Know the Differences Between Needs, Desires, and Goals

How many times have you gone shopping and exclaimed *"I need this!"* about something you didn't really need? Probably many times. Whether the object of desire is shoes, a toy, a stereo system, or a new piece of gaming equipment, it's doubtful that you would really need it. You might want it badly, but wanting something a lot does not necessarily equate to needing it.

Most people in developed countries have similar material needs. We won't delve too much into Maslow's hierarchy of needs and self-actualization; instead, we will keep it focused on the physical[2] (Mcleod, 2020). We need a roof over our heads; for example, renting versus owning is an expression of desire—not need. We need enough food to nourish ourselves, along with clothing.

To live in the modern world, we need other things as well. If you live in an area without good public transportation, you will probably need a car to get around. You need electricity and an Internet connection, which would certainly come as a surprise to your great-great-grandfather! The reality is that the modern world creates certain demands that we must abide by to function. You need a phone, though technically a smartphone specifically isn't necessary.

Nearly everything else is a "want." There are tons of *wants* we could go over—wanting to hang out with friends and eat nachos at a sports bar, wanting to go to professional sports games, wanting to own a pet, wanting a state-of-the-art stereo or video game system, or wanting the latest smartphone are all *wants* that you don't necessarily *need*. You may want to browse storefronts or check online stores; however, you don't need to spend money on what you see.

We live in a consumerist society, and we signal our values with what we buy. Although we do need clothing, we don't necessarily need to purchase designer clothes. Expensive designers are a want, not a need. Vehicles are necessary; however, most people don't really need giant SUVs or gas-guzzling pickup trucks, nor do we need that brand new car. Those are desires and ways to show others what's important to us.

What's necessary for most people is just a boring old two or four-door car that has good gas mileage. This year's smartphone is pretty much exactly the same as last year's. Maybe the company added a pixel on the camera, or some other feature that's more or less irrelevant to how you use it. No matter how many new add-ons they implement, you don't actually need to upgrade; you just want to.

Your needs are probably already covered. What was the last thing you wanted to buy? Would you even have room for it? Did you have enough money on hand to pay for it, or did you plan to add it to your credit card and increase the amount of money you owe exponentially? (We'll discuss compound interest shortly).

Think about what your values are, which is probably not mindless shopping. Nevertheless, maybe you're big into the environment and saving the planet. Very few items that you buy will be good for the environment unless you're buying a new energy-efficient washing machine or other similar products.

Is it important to you to spend time with your friends? Hopefully, it is! We humans are naturally social beings, but you don't have to spend tons of money to do that. If that's why you were spending so much money on happy hour, it's easy enough to stop. Invite your buddies over and tell them to bring their own drinks. It's much cheaper to buy from the store instead of paying the markup when you go out, and you can still have more fun at home than at the bar anyway!

Can't go out due to the coronavirus? Consider trying FaceTime, Skype, Zoom, or whatever other similar services are out there. Through video calling, you can still have a virtual party with your friends. You can then switch to house parties once the pandemic is over and restrictions are lifted. I personally expect that people will get used to these new ways of socializing, which will likely become the new norm.

Is fitness important to you? Great! But do you have to join the fanciest and most expensive gym in town? Not necessarily. Instead, try setting up your own gym. Find a cheaper place you can go to when the restrictions are lifted and watch some how-to work out and set up videos online.

For pretty much anything you value, there will be other ways to enjoy it without having to pay so much money. You may argue it's just $20 a month. Although that may be correct, $20 per month turns into $240 per year, or $4,800 after 20 years (not including interest). If you're in the 22% tax bracket here in the US, you would have had to earn over $6,100 to save that much! How valuable is $240 per year during crisis time? Clearly it does have quite a big value.

Spending is the easiest and most mindless way to express your values. Let's try something different.

What are your goals in life? Everyone should be thinking about retirement because you need to save up your own money to avoid being poverty-stricken in old age. No, you won't be able to work forever—at some point, you will no longer be physically or mentally able to work 40 hours a week. Decline starts earlier than most people think, and financial literacy starts dropping at age 60[3] (Finke et al., 2016).

If retirement is the goal, what else might you want to do? Buy a house, stop working for someone else and run your own business? Travel? Write those ideas down. Knowing why you want to cut back on spending (besides cutting back during the coronavirus crisis) will help you get through the times when the short term beckons with cute shoes or powerful game equipment.

I have written a new book *Work from Home During and After the Economic Crisis* that is complementary to this one. It describes how to earn money as a freelancer or entrepreneur during this crisis and fix your other problem: lack of income. For starting any business, you will need some initial "seed" money to pay your bills until you're profitable. On the other hand, investing in your own business will bear the highest return because you won't have to share that profit with anyone else.

Consequences of Saving vs. Spending

OK, we might need a little math when figuring out our expenses, but we'll keep it simple. Compound interest is something that you cannot control. You can either learn to use it to your advantage or suffer by having others, like credit card companies, use it against you.

Compound interest is basically money growing on itself. If, for example, you have $1,000 that earns a 10% return annually, at the end of one year, you would have $1,100. Then, in the next year, the 10% grows on top of that $1,100; not the original $1,000, and so forth. It takes a little while for compounding to hit its stride— years, not months. Therefore, leaving your money alone can be pretty powerful. Consider a more reasonable scenario in which your $1,000 is earning an average 6% return, as it would if invested in a portfolio that contained more stocks than bonds.

Get to know the Rule of 72, which tells you how long the money takes to double, given a specific return. In the example above, your $1,000 would turn into $2,000 at the end of twelve years (72/6 = 12). Doesn't sound too impressive? Try $10,000. In twelve years, that amount would become $20,000 without you adding to it or even doing anything. You were merely staying away from it and letting it grow. While you can't control the average return of your portfolio, you can influence it by being proactive, which would mean adding stocks.

If you earned 8% on average with an all-stock portfolio, your money would double in 9 years instead of 12. If you left it for 36 years, it would double four times. At a 6% return, it would double only three times.

You also control the time you leave your money to compound for you. It's a good idea to start early and not panic and sell off your stocks when a recession hits. Right now, bonds generate maybe about 3%, which means it would take 24 years to double. If everything's in cash, you will not be earning anything. There would be no compounding at all, and certainly no doubling.

Now, imagine this power working against you. In that case, you would start with a $1,000 debt, which would probably be on your credit cards (student loans and mortgages don't compound in the same way that credit cards do). You wouldn't pay it off. Typical credit cards compound about 24% annually, and your $1,000, if you don't pay it off right away, would be $2,000 in three years. That is all assuming you don't add to it... which is unlikely.

If you have credit card debt, one of your first goals should be to pay it off as soon as you can. Right now during the crisis, doing so may not be possible. Afterward, however, you can do your best to keep your spending cuts in place and use the savings to pay off credit cards and create an emergency fund.

This **emergency fund** will prevent you from adding back to your credit card debt if something were to happen. You need three to six months' expenses in cash in that fund, depending on your situation and how much risk you're comfortable taking (Elkins, 2019).[4]

How Much Are You Spending?

Right now, you may not even recognize just how much you are spending. If you're living paycheck to paycheck, spending your income (other than contributions you make for your savings, including retirement), and using credit cards and not paying them off at the end of the month, it means your spending exceeds your income. In either case, you definitely need to cut back, but where would you do that?

First, you need to know where your money is going. There are many online apps that can help you do the tracking without lifting a finger (LaPonsie, 2019).[5] There is little difference between all of them, so pick one that's free and start using it right away.

Search through your current statements to see where your past few months' spending has gone. Some of your expenses may be on necessities such as rent or mortgage, utilities, and groceries. We will be going over proven tips on reducing costs surrounding those too in a bit. Nevertheless, most people find it easier to attack the discretionary items that they want but don't need: mindless shopping, entertainment, and eating out to name a few examples.

Look through how much you spend on your *wants*. Which of these wants match up with what you value, and which of them were just mindless spending? For example, suppose you value spending time with friends, but your credit card statements reveal that you spend often at the priciest clothes store in town or at the game store. You can cut those expenses out without feeling deprived because time with friends is what's important to you.

You may find that some of these expenses are nothing more than habits, and that staying home during the coronavirus might break you of them without you having to do too much! Maybe you were in the habit of going to the local coffee shop during your afternoon break for a little pick-me-up. Now that you are no longer working in your office, you don't need to hit that coffee shop. You might still need a little something in the afternoon, but you can make your own coffee at home without all the sugar and additives. You can also decide to take some time to stretch and breathe deeply, which can be enough to keep you going.

In other words, the key is to only spend money on the things you value (we'll talk about ways to spend less money on them without feeling deprived in the ensuing chapters). No more mindlessly throwing down the credit card for anything that catches your eye. You'll think about your purchases before you make them. Best of all, you'll be enjoying yourself without feeling too deprived, as it is important to feel good, even more so in difficult times. Such will help you continue your new, better habits once the coronavirus is under control.

Chapter Summary

- Mindset and taking control of things that you can influence are important for managing your money.
- Knowing your goals and understanding the difference between wants and needs will help you tackle your spending.
- Compound interest is to your advantage when you use it for savings, but works against you when you incur debt, especially on credit cards.
- Track your spending to figure out what's mindless and can be cut.

In the next chapter, you will learn some tips for cutting back on your food expenses, both in terms of eating out and groceries.

---

[1] Emotional Intelligence: Why It Can Matter More Than IQ, by Daniel Goleman

[2] https://www.simplypsychology.org/maslow.html

[3] https://pubsonline.informs.org/doi/10.1287/mnsc.2015.2293

[4] https://www.cnbc.com/2019/10/18/minimum-amount-of-money-you-need-in-an-emergency-fund.html

[5] https://money.usnews.com/money/personal-finance/saving-and-budgeting/articles/best-expense-tracker-apps

Chapter **TWO**

FOCUS ON FOOD

REMEMBER the difference between wants and needs when thinking about food! You need nourishment to survive, but eating out or buying luxury items is a want. You may value the quality of your food, which means avoiding processed foods and often buying local or organic, but it's important to note that these kinds of food is more expensive than processed or fast food, which is OK. You just need to be cognizant of the trade-offs you need to make.

Cooking your own food at home is usually cheaper than going out to eat, unless you've been living on the dollar menu at the fast-food chains. However, your health is important too, and eating mainly fast food will lead to health issues down the road.

Remember to consider both nutritional value and dollar value when eating out. Much of the food in restaurants—especially in fast food and fast-casual restaurants—are loaded with calories.

However, they don't provide nourishment, which is what your

body really needs. This food tends to be low in the fiber, vitamins, and minerals that you would get from unprocessed foods you can cook yourself. Even in high-end restaurants, the food is often slathered in butter and cream that you don't need.

The demands of your day may require that you eat out on occasion. You can still save money and eat good food when you do so, as long as you're mindful about it. Sometimes, you may just want to treat yourself, which is OK too, as long as it's not a daily or even weekly thing.

During the coronavirus crisis, you will probably end up spending more time cooking at home anyway, so that's a bonus! While you're doing it, find fun ways to make things that you like to eat which will provide you the nourishment you need. Then, once we're able to go back to the restaurants, you'll be satisfied with going out as a treat and making the most of your meals at home. You will learn what you like to cook and master the ingredients list, which will help you cut down on grocery spending.

You may have some cookbooks lying around, and now would be a great time to pull them out and dust them off. See what looks interesting and works with what you have on hand. Whether or not you've got cookbooks, the Internet is your friend during the crisis! You can find all kinds of recipes online, and even if you are someone who prefers to watch, there are plenty of videos on preparing food too. You might end up a master onion slicer by the end of the crisis!

Quick Tips to Start Now

The following are all things you can do right this moment to save money on food. Bring this book into the kitchen with you and get going!

o Shop your pantry

Most of us have a ton of things we bought because they looked interesting, or we planned to make a meal we didn't end up cooking. In other cases, something was on sale, so we ended up scooping it up but never using it. Therefore, it's a great idea to delve into the backs of your cupboard and dig out whatever's lurking back there.

Some cans or boxes may have expiration dates. If it does and you're well past the date, toss it. Saving money is not worth getting sick! Some staples like beans can last almost for forever.

What kind of meal can you make with these items? Depending on the variety, you might not have any idea! It's time to whip out the cookbooks. Look in the index for an ingredient to see what you can come up with, or search online for a recipe.

o Switch to water for drinking

Up to 60% of the human body is actually water. Your brain and heart are both mostly composed of water, and all your other organs, including skin and bones, have water in them, which means it's crucial to stay hydrated. It's also a great way to avoid kidney stones. Your body and brain also function better when they get enough water.

It gets even cheaper when you stop buying gallons of soda. You also don't need sugar or artificial sweetener if you drink diet soda. Artificial sweeteners play a trick on your body, and people can become addicted to the sweet taste. However, because there are no calories, your body thinks it's still hungry. That's when you start scanning the shelves (or your cupboards) for something sweet and comforting, and end up consuming more calories.

This is partially the reason why we have so many overweight people in the US; despite their use of dieting, they buy soda with no sugar or other drinks with sweeteners. It would require an entire book to explain why most diets do not work in the long term. Sweet drinks, whether sweetened with sugar or a no-calorie substitute, are a major factor. Fortunately, these sweetening agents can be easily removed, especially when you're trying to save money.

Fruit juice isn't necessary or even all that healthy for you. Packaged juice doesn't contain the natural vitamins of the fruit, and the added vitamins aren't very effective. Eat the whole fruit instead. One apple may have just a little vitamin C, but it will give you more than the juice with added vitamins.

This doesn't mean that you should go out and hoard cases of bottled water! In most cases, the water is simply bottled tap water, which is nothing special. Not only are you adding to the plastic waste that's destroying the earth and its oceans, but you're overpaying for it.

Drink tap water if you can—this means doing so unless you live in one of the handful of municipalities where the water is contaminated and unsafe to drink, such as Flint, Michigan. If you don't like the taste of your tap, buy a filter. Researchers conducted tests in which people compared bottled and tap water from unmarked glasses. Tap water finished among the top three in terms of taste almost every time.

Yes, I said to buy something! But the reality is that, over time, if you drink filtered water, it will end up being cheaper than buying sodas or bottled water. If you don't like cold water, then leave it at room temperature. Chill your water if you don't like it warm, and infuse it with fruit, lemons, or limes to add a little taste if you like.

○ **Make your coffee or tea at home**

Going out to the coffee shop may be convenient, but it is way more expensive compared to just making it at home. You don't need a specialty coffee or frappe every day.

If you've been completely reliant on coffee shops to date, you may have to buy a coffee maker or a kettle and learn to brew the coffee yourself. Again, there's an upfront cost, but you'll end up spending less over time by making your own, which will repay your investment in a month or two. You may even already have one somewhere in your house, and now wouldn't be a bad time to pull it out from the back of the cupboard where you stashed it and dust it off.

You can buy bags of beans at the grocery store once you go through whatever bags you already have at home. It tastes best if you buy whole beans and grind what you need just before you brew it. If you're not into that, bags of ground coffee are also fine. Just seal the bags after using to keep coffee fresh. Once you learn how to make good coffee, and our society goes back to normal, you can invite your friends over for tasting.

If you're more of a tea fan, you can buy tea bags or loose tea and get your tea fix. I like to have a combination of caffeinated and herbal—that way, I can have a cup of herbal tea late in the afternoon for a little pick-me-up and not have to worry about whether I'll be able to sleep that night!

○ **Grocery shop with a list**

After you've gone pantry shopping, you may still need to pick up a few other items at the store, or you need to replace some food once you've cleaned out your pantry and made meals out of what you had lying around. Don't go hungry because you won't be able to control yourself! Also, don't go without a list.

Get into the habit of looking at the contents of your fridge and pantry before you go grocery shopping. Check what you have already to make sure you don't overbuy.

When you get to the grocery store, your mission is to buy *only* what's on your list. If the shelves seem to empty quickly, they will be refilled. Once the pandemic panic has passed, the shelves will quickly fill up again. Now is a good time to practice only buying what's on your list!

o Grocery shop online and pick-up at the store

Having a hard time sticking to your list? As long as your store offers curbside pickup for free, go ahead and use that. It's especially helpful during this time of crisis, because you can stay isolated at home and avoid going into a store and coming in contact with many people all at once.

Shop online, then go pick it up. It's easy, healthy, and less subject to temptation!

o If you need to order out, order takeout

Ordering takeout may be a little less convenient, but delivery services are expensive, even without the tips, so avoid them whenever possible. You don't need to pay the surcharge if you can call ahead and go to the restaurant to pick your food up yourself.

o If you're sick right now...

Some of these tips won't work if you're sick, whether you have the coronavirus or another virus, like the common cold or flu. Stay home and avoid spreading those germs if you can. If you don't have enough food from pantry shopping, then opt to get food delivered to you. Better yet, if you ask a friend, neighbor, or relative to get the food for you, so you don't have to pay the delivery charge. They can leave it at your door, so they don't get sick too. **175**

Medium-Term Tips to Implement Within the Next Few Months

These tricks may require you to spend a little bit more time thinking about your plan. Otherwise, they may take a bit more time to implement.

- **Plan your meals at least weekly**

  Planning ahead of time means fewer nights of ordering takeout out of exhaustion and lack of food at home. It also makes grocery shopping more relaxed, because you know exactly what you need to buy for the meals you're making. It also cuts down on overbuying.

  Work around the events coming up in your life. If you have a couple nights that you know you will be working late, you may opt to buy frozen meals. They may not be that great for you, so a better idea would be to have meals prepped on, say, Sunday night, which you can then heat up easily throughout the week. If you know you have a happy hour or client lunch that week, you won't have to buy anything for those meals. Right now, you probably do need to plan on cooking them all at home!

- **DIY your food prep**

  When you go to the grocery store, it's certainly possible to buy vegetables and fruits that are already cut up into sticks or cubes for you. Many stores even have their own salad bars, which are almost comically overpriced compared to the amount of meals you could make buying the ingredients themselves. You can buy an already roasted chicken or packages of uncooked chicken pieces such as breasts, thighs, and drumsticks.

  Know that you're paying for someone else to do this prep for you. Buying a bunch of whole carrots will provide you with much more carrot for your buck than investing in a little container of carrot sticks.

Instead of paying someone to do the prep for you, cut both your costs and your vegetables. If you know you've got a busy week ahead, prep the food when you get home from the store. Prepping your food will entail slicing your carrots and peppers, washing your salad greens if you have a salad spinner, etc.

The most economic way to get chicken is to buy a whole one and roast it. You can portion out the meat and save the bones for stock. Make sure to use up the whole chicken. It's more flavorful when you cook it with the bones in instead of un-wrapping a plastic-wrapped, pale chicken breast that's had the skin and bones removed.

- **Buy in bulk when you can**

Not everything can be bought in bulk—fresh vegetables, for example, go bad pretty quickly! However, pantry staples like beans, canned tomatoes, pasta, and rice can be kept more or less indefinitely.

When you have perishable items or those that go bad fairly quickly after opening, consider whether you can freeze what you're not using. For example, when meat is on sale at the grocery store, portion it out and freeze the extra for later. But remember—any unfrozen food cannot be frozen again, but must be consumed quickly.

- **Eating out? Go to happy hour**

Right now during the coronavirus crisis, you may not be doing a lot of eating out, other than takeout. Reducing the number of meals you have away from home will be great for your wallet! However, there may be times when you can't 177 convince everyone to potluck and bring their own drinks to your house. Otherwise, you may need a little bit of a treat after work.

Hit up happy hour (or lunch) rather than dinner. Both choices are almost always less expensive compared to dinner, and you may not necessarily be in the mood for the massive dinner portions that many restaurants tend to serve during those hours. Happy hour is often more fun within a more relaxed setting.

o Eating out? Order appetizers or share entrees

In some cases, you may not be able to make it to happy hour, or the people you're dining with insist on a more formal meal. Despite these changes in the plan, you still don't have to pay an arm and a leg to have a nice dinner. Appetizers give you a chance to try something new with smaller portions. Often, choosing two appetizers for dinner will still cost you less than having a single entree. Another option when eating with a friend is to share an entree. Most restaurant portions are quite a bit larger than you would really need, and sharing is a great way to fix that.

Either way, if you don't finish all the food, box it up to go. If it's not enough for a full portion, you can still pair the food with a little something you have at home for lunch the next day. If it's protein, make a salad to accompany it, and if it's vegetables, throw an egg on top. Get creative and don't let anything go to waste.

o Watch the booze

Alcohol is an enormous moneymaker for restaurants, and the markup is insane for wine and spirits. Wine by the glass is almost always a hefty surcharge, compared to buying a bottle at the wine store. You could try going to a place where you can bring your own, though some charge a "corkage fee" to open it for you.

If you plan to drink while you're out, be smart and wallet-wise about it. Have a glass of water in between each alcoholic drink, which can help prevent you from getting drunk too quickly. It will also cut down on the amount of overpriced booze you're drinking, ultimately reducing your costs.

Long-Term Planning

What does saving money mean when you're looking out for the long term? After the crisis is over, we will be able to sit and enjoy restaurants again. Hopefully, you can use this time now to develop good habits of cooking at home and save when eating out for treats and special occasions.

o **Develop a menu of the dishes you'll cook and rotate them**

If you don't need a lot of variety in your food, this tip will work exceptionally well for you. If you do need variety, you will need a larger menu of items, including for breakfast, lunch, and dinner. You don't have to make dinner a big meal or production, so you may choose to use the same recipes for both lunch and dinner, though not on the same day.

When at home cooking because you can't go out, you gain the opportunity to try different meals. Some may not be worth the effort (or clean-up) that you would have to put in, whereas others might be quick and terrific. Find the ones you like to make and eat, then you can rotate them throughout the week. You'll know exactly the ingredients you need, and how much you need, which will keep costs down and help prevent you from buying too much.

You do need some variety, so make sure you're not making dishes in which potatoes are the only vegetable, for example. You can incorporate plant-based foods in, if you haven't already. **179**

Set aside non-meat times, like Meatless Mondays, since making meals from beans and other plant-based proteins will be cheaper than buying meat.

You might have different dishes that you will want to eat throughout the different seasons. Maybe you love meatloaf, but you save that for winter time and put sloppy joes in the summer rotation. In another case, you might rotate the same protein dishes all year, but switch out the vegetables and fruits according to season.

At the end of the day, it is *your* menu! *You* get to eat what's nutritious and tasty for you and your household. Don't like beets? Don't put them in your rotation. Don't like brussels sprouts? Don't use them, but do add in broccoli and/or cauliflower since they contain similar nutrients.

o **Preserve**

During the summer, fruit trees are laden with fruit and are quite cheap! Consider learning how to preserve your summer fruits and veggies to enjoy later on in the year and to prevent waste.

Make jellies and jams and shrubs with your fruit. You can also pickle your fruit veggies. Don't let the abundance of zucchini go to waste!

Another option is fermented food, which is great for your gut, so consider making your own sauerkraut and kimchi. It won't be much work on your part, and you won't need any fancy starters either.

o **Shop seasonally**

Sure, you can buy strawberries and tomatoes in December, but *ugh*! Why would you want to? Fruits and veggies that are out of season are expensive, and they don't taste very good either.

When it's spring, buy your spring produce: berries, asparagus, and peas. In the summer, go for corn, summer squash like zucchini, and citrus. In the fall, you can enjoy apples and pears, along with the start of winter squashes. These fall produce options will also carry you through winter, with some of the cold-weather lettuces.

If you're buying at the farmer's market, think about going late. The potential downside to doing so is that, if you're shopping for something specific, there may not be any left by the time you get there! However, if you're just looking for products in general and don't need anything specific, you might still find some great bargains. The farmers prefer not to haul the food back with them, so they might give you discounts at the end of the day.

Chapter Summary

- Although food is a necessity of life, you can find ways to reduce how much you're spending on it by eating more at home and buying judiciously.
- You can implement some suggestions quickly, like "shopping" your pantry, using a list when you go grocery shopping, and drinking water instead of pricey soda or fruit drinks.
- In the medium term, do your meal planning weekly and manage costs of eating out by going out for happy hour or splitting entrees.
- Long-term steps include creating a menu of dishes that you would rotate and shopping seasonally.
- You can save several thousands of dollars a year just by managing your food.

In the next chapter, we will go over how you can reduce your household costs, such as in utilities and rent.

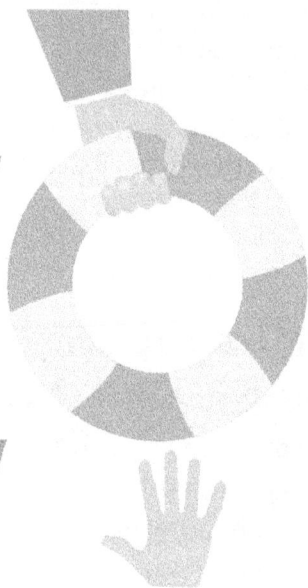

SAVE MONEY AND SPEND WISELY

Chapter **THREE**

PANDEMIC-PROOF YOUR HOME COSTS

WE tend to think of housing costs as fixed costs: the mortgage or rent is a certain amount, and the utilities are what they are. However, there are several methods that you can use right now to drop these supposedly fixed costs. Housing is a big-ticket item, and if you can reduce these costs using the tips provided below, you'll end up saving a lot of money. In the short term, there are smaller changes you can make that can really add up once you start implementing them (remember that the $20 you're saving is the equivalent to your having to earn over $6,100!)

Quick Tips to Start Now

o **Adjust your thermostats to use less energy**

   Did you know that you don't have to set your thermostat so that you're perfectly comfortable in a t-shirt and shorts (or sweatshirt and sweatpants), no matter the weather outside? By letting your home be a little warmer in the summer and a little cooler in the winter, you can save quite a bit of money.

The US Department of Energy estimates that nearly half of your home energy consumption is due to heating and cooling costs (Crank, 2018)[6] You will see that reducing these costs right away will make a big difference in your savings. Adjusting just 1° over eight hours can save you 1% on your bills. Multiply that by multiple degrees during the day and watch those savings grow.

In the winter, when you decrease the temperature at which your heat comes on, you can wear sweaters, sweatshirts, or warm robes so you stay warm, even when your heat hasn't come on yet. If you have ceiling fans, you can actually use those to help heat the rooms. Flip the switch so the blades rotate in a different direction, and the fan will push the warmer air at the top of the room down toward where you are.

In the summer, you'll need to flip the switch back, so the fan can once again provide a cooling breeze. Doing so will allow you to avoid turning your air conditioning (a/c) on. You might also want to try turning your desk and floor fans on to cool you off. Your location will determine whether your heating or your a/c system will be more expensive for you to run; however, you can reduce costs for both.

- **Refinance your mortgage and bank wisely**

Now, while interest rates are low, may be a great time for you to consider refinancing your mortgage, especially if you've been able to increase the amount of equity in your home. It's definitely worth it to reach out to your mortgage professional. They may not be working in their offices during the pandemic, but most mortgage-related documentation is now done digitally, so you may still be able to contact them. Find out how much you can save on your monthly payment now, though beware of closing costs and points. However, do not spend all your cash and keep that emergency fund we described in chapter 10.

You'll definitely want to have your rational thinking hat on when comparing the numbers and deciding if—after all the costs and fees—it makes sense. You might be able to squeeze out some extra points in your benefit if the mortgage companies are looking to do some business during this cash crunch time.

This will be the same with your banking, and you might need to do a little research to figure out how much you can save while banking. However, sheltering in place will be the perfect time to do it. You may find banks that are offering discounts on fees or reducing other costs during the coronavirus pandemic—use them! These advantages and benefits will probably not be offered once the coronavirus is back under control, so don't delay. They will not stick around for long.

o **Using the dishwasher vs. hand washing dishes**

It's actually more energy efficient to use your dishwasher compared to hand washing dishes; that is, if you have a newer model washer. If your model was built before 2013, and especially if it's pre-2000, you may be better off continuing your hand washing (Bradford, 2017).[7]

It may seem counter-intuitive because the dishwasher uses electricity; however, you may not realize that hand washing does too because using the sink also means using your hot-water heater. Newer dishwashers heat water more efficiently than your hot-water heater does, which helps to save energy on a full load of dishes.

Many people don't pay for water usage, but newer dishwashers are much more efficient with water than you would be washing in the sink. With hand washing, you may use up to 27 gallons washing the same load of dishes it would take your dishwasher to clean with about 3 gallons, which is a *massive* difference. If you don't pay for water, consider how much you're saving the earth too!

There are also ways to make your dishwasher even more efficient, and running full loads is one of them. Use vinegar for the rinse, then cut back on energy use by letting dishes air dry instead of using the heat dry option. If there is excess food on the plate, scrape it into the trash or compost and don't rinse before you put it in.

o Shop home insurance and consider bundling

How much is your premium for home or renter's insurance? This is another bill that can be pretty hefty! While you're at home, go online or call different insurance agencies to see if you can get a better deal.

Calling is often a great way to get a better deal because human agents are much more susceptible to your threats of leaving if they can't give you that better deal! Also, consider if you're better off bundling your car insurance. Many insurance companies will give you a better deal if you combine your home or renter's policy with your vehicle.

As always, remember to read the fine print carefully and make sure you're not accepting reduced coverage in an effort to reduce your costs. Also, ensure any trade-offs you're making are worth it—you may get a lower monthly payment in exchange for a higher deductible, which means you would be paying more out of pocket if an incident does occur. If you can't come up with the higher deductible amount, you may need to accept a higher monthly payment.

Medium-Term Tips to Implement Within the Next Few Months

As you can see, there are plenty of ways that you can reduce the costs you may have previously thought were fixed. You can do the ones we discussed above right away. However, those aren't the only tips I'm offering. In the next few months, even after you've adjusted your thermostats and taken advantage of the short-term cuts, you can still continue to drive your home costs down.

- **Choose energy-efficient products when it's time to replace**

  When you're renting, some landlords will provide things like refrigerators and washing machines, but there are many who don't. In these cases, you may also need to replace a microwave or other small appliances. If you're a homeowner, you'll definitely need to replace these items over time, in addition to larger expenses like roofs, windows and doors.

  As stated, appliances and other household items wear out over time and will need to be replaced. Some last longer than others, but it's likely that you will have to buy new things after a while. When you're replacing all these items, you don't need the most expensive or flashiest new model; for example, if you're a household of two people, there's no reason to buy a washing machine that can handle loads for a household of six. Match the appliance to your own usage.

  The other important factor in replacement is its energy efficiency. If you have an older model and think it may have another year in it, research perks that would come from newer models. If you've got something that's ten years old or older, the newer models will likely save you a lot more money just through energy efficiency. For example, replacing your old washing machine with a newer model that uses half energy and half water can save you a lot over the next year.

Your home's insulation can make a huge difference in your heating and cooling costs. If your weatherstripping is old or nonexistent, you may be losing a lot of energy to the great outdoors. Make sure that your replacement doors and windows are energy efficient.

If you live in a hotter climate, your window dressing can actually save you money as well. Mini blinds can't do much for you, but you can buy sunlight-blocking sheers and blackout curtains to darken the room. They are great for sleeping and saving money on a/c when the sun can't heat the room as well.

o **Do housework for the landlord in exchange for rent reduction**

There is a lot of work that goes into keeping up a property. Landlords need to keep their place looking nice to attract good tenants. With all the upkeep required, you may be able to make a tradeoff for them, so they don't have to spend money on gardeners or exterior painters.

If there's a laundry room or other common area, it needs to be kept clean. See if your cleaning abilities can help with your rent! Either way, you can at least try this tactic to avoid a rent increase.

o **Save money with lights**

If it's hard to remember to turn the lights off when you've finished your business in a room, it may be a good idea to install occupancy sensors. Infrared sensors work on heat and motion and turn the lights on when someone's in the room. They will also turn them off when they no longer detect heat or movement. Outside, motion-activated lights will work well on your front door and elsewhere, placed strategically for your protection.

You can also consider dimming your lights, which would save you energy and make your modern light bulbs last longer. Dim lights require less energy, and dimmers are great for rooms or 189 hallways that you don't use all the time, but where you might need some light at night. Dimming doesn't work as well for old-school incandescent use, as it shortens their typical lifespan.

Both LED and compact fluorescents (CFLs) are more energy efficient than incandescent bulbs. You'll want to make sure you choose the right color LED for the room. Those on the lower end of the light spectrum create a warmer, cozier light, whereas those at the higher end are clearer and brighter. High spectrum lights are well suited for task or office lighting, though you may want a cozier, warmer glow in the bedroom.

o **Use smart power strips**

When items like computers and televisions are plugged in, they consume a little energy even while turned off. Smart power strips manage the electricity that goes to each outlet on the strip to maximize energy efficiency, and all might shut off if there's no activity on the strip for a while.

When the main item is shut off, all the others associated with it would also be shut off. For example, suppose you have a television set with a game console, streaming stick, and soundbar associated with it. When you shut off the TV with a smart strip, the console, stick, and bar shut down too. For your wifi router, there may be an "always on" socket.

o **Consider housemates or short-term rentals**

As noted above, rent and mortgage are significant expenses. You can slash them along with utility bills by sharing the cost with someone else. If you have an unused room, think about renting it out to a housemate or for short-term rental.

Although you may feel a bit nervous at sharing your place long-term, it seems unlikely that short-term rentals will bounce back right away after the coronavirus crisis has ended. Many people haven't been able to work, so vacation plans will probably be put on hold in the future.

By the same token, plenty of people will probably need to cut back on expenses whenever they can, just like you. Just as a side, it will likely be easier to find a roommate than it will be to find someone to rent for the short term. Be active, look around, and post on social media.

Make sure you know what your landlord or housing association will accept! Protect yourself legally in case you run into a problem with your roommate not paying, which may mean they will have to be put on the lease so the landlord can evict them. That protection will also assure your association or town won't fine you for short-term rentals.

o Reduce, reuse, recycle, upcycle

While it's true that energy-consuming home items and materials are most energy-efficient when they're new, that's not necessarily true for everything in your home. A brand new chair won't be more energy-efficient than your old chair, and it may be even worse for the environment, since modern manufacturing methods are known to cause damage to the earth.

So, when it comes to furniture and dishes, for example, instead of upgrading and buying a newer version, don't be afraid to get creative. Trust me—if there's anything you want to do around the house, there will probably be a video or graphic tutorial online that will teach you how to do it!

If you're tired of the way your chairs look, reupholster them using materials you have lying around. Try your hand at needle-crafting if you require new napkins, tablecloths, placemats, or wall hangings. You can also take an old nightstand and create a desk out of it.

Although a professional could probably do the work for you, the money going to them could be placed somewhere else instead. Professionals use new materials, and repair costs may be close to the price of a new item. If you cannot repair it properly, at least prolong its life with smaller, quick, and easy fixes.

You can reuse chipped glasses as toothbrush mugs or pencil holders. Old dishes you don't like can sit under your plants and catch the water and heavy bowls you don't like can be repurposed for feeding and watering pets. For cleaning rags, cut up, old, and stained t-shirts. They will also be good for wiping down your electronics. You can wash your rags in your energy-efficient washing machine. On the other hand, if you do need to use paper towels, challenge yourself to make that paper towel roll last as long as possible!

What do you have lying around in your cupboards or crammed into the back of your drawers? If you can't think of anything for any miscellaneous items you find, see what shows up on a quick internet search. You might be surprised.

o **Plan furniture buying ahead of time**

When you go impulse shopping, for anything—food, clothes, and furniture, for example—you tend to spend more money than you should. In those cases, you may not even end up with something you genuinely like because you felt pressured into buying that item.

Planning ahead of time allows you to budget and save up the amount you need. Thus, you wouldn't need to worry about having interest work against you; instead, buy it for cash or put it on a credit card for points but pay the debt off immediately.

Thrift and consignment stores are your friend, and you may find some cheap, badly used particleboard nonsense. Chances are, you'll find some furniture with patterns that are absolutely hideous, and no one decorates their homes like the 1980s anymore for a reason. However, you'll also find furniture built out of solid materials that were made to last and consider what's underneath the hideous pattern. Is the frame well-made? You can always reupholster a nightmare fabric if it's located on a beautiful frame that was built to last.

Giving yourself time to buy also means you can spend some time looking. You may also be able to strike a deal, particularly in a thrift store where the owner needs space for new stuff regularly.

Long-term planning

Even more money can be saved over the long term with planning and questioning. Many of us tend to stick with decisions once we've made them, even as circumstances change; however, what was the best for us and our families five years ago may no longer be the optimal choice. Now's a good time to question whether where we're living is still the right place for us and, if so, how we can make it sustainable and less expensive through the coming years.

o Smart and efficient major renovations

Where you are right now can be a great place in terms of neighborhood and environment. You may not want to make any changes in location in the near future. However, your house itself may need some major changes to accommodate your needs. You upcycled and recycled as much as you could, but now you're looking at larger structural changes for your home.

As with any big home project, make sure you get plenty of bids for the work and do your homework. With every major change, think about energy efficiency in your projects and how the proposed changes will affect your heating and cooling bills. If you live in a hotter climate, maybe a glass-enclosed atrium facing   **193** west isn't a great idea! Ensure that the windows you're planning will be well-insulated.

How will the roof of a new addition fit with your existing roof, and how will it handle the heat and rain? If you're opening up space indoors by taking down walls, how does that affect your HVAC and electrical systems? These are all questions you need to consider while reworking your home. Big changes can make your house feel completely new! With every renovation, make a goal to improve your energy efficiency.

- **Consider buying a fixer-upper if in the hunt for a new house**

If you're looking for a new home, you'll need to do some math if you want to get the most out of every penny. Most neighborhoods usually have a mix of older and newer homes, so you won't immediately be comparing apples to apples.

The older homes may be well-cared-for, fixer-uppers, or a mix of both. At first glance, the fixer-uppers would look the most economical, and they may very well be! However, you'll need to take the calculator out to make sure. What energy-efficient upgrades will you need to make on your chosen fixer-upper? Often, you'll need to replace the windows and, perhaps, the doors. How much work will the inside take? Even the handiest people should hire an electrician for the wiring. Don't forget to add dimmers and occupancy sensors if necessary.

Your creativity in recycling and upcycling will come in handy here. The great thing about fixer-uppers is that, when renovating, you get to make the house exactly the way you want it. Keep in mind that older homes that have been maintained better may be more expensive to start with, and you may still need to do some work to make sure they're energy-efficient. It may need a new roof, windows, and doors. When comparing with a brand new house, do your research to figure out how efficient it really is. Does it have upgraded, efficient features? It may be new, but efficiency is no guarantee!

Energy efficiency is often overlooked because people focus on the purchase price. At this point now, however, you can recognize how the overall price would also include utilities and necessary renovations. These can be strong arguments when negotiating price.

o How big a home do you really need?

Just as you don't need a washing machine that handles the filth of six people when there's only two of you in the house, it's not necessary to buy a large house when you don't plan to fill it with people.

There are many benefits to buying a house that's only as big as you need it to be, and no bigger. Smaller houses are more energy efficient. You also don't have as many rooms to heat, cool, light, and clean.

In general, they're also quite a bit cheaper upfront, at least when you're comparing houses that are in similar locations. A house out in the suburbs of a major city may appear cheaper at first compared to a smaller condo downtown in that same city. The reason it only appears so at first is because, after looking at initial costs, you would have to factor in the commute and associated costs that come with that.

o Smaller house prices may be cheaper this year (2020)

Recessions tend to depress housing markets too, though certain markets are relatively immune to stock market drops. However, home builders, recognizing the need to house millennials, are building more entry-level homes, so you might get lucky!

195

○ Move to a less expensive suburb

Some US cities are becoming too expensive to live in, so you may need to move to a suburb anyway. You will notice that certain suburbs are more affordable than others. Remember to be mindful about your purchase.

Therefore, you don't need to move to the most chic, hipster suburb for your city. Instead, broaden your scope. Other neighborhoods may not look as cool and you might have to walk farther to the shops that you need, but if it's cheaper, you should consider it!

The price of housing goes hand in hand with other living expenses. In higher end suburbs, you may see some of your neighbors having a higher standard of living. Your children might meet wealthier schoolmates daily, and they may find it difficult to cope with the differences. Often, we compare our lives with others unconsciously when making important decisions. If your neighbors just bought a brand new car and took an expensive vacation, how will you feel if you can't afford to do the same?

On the other hand, a neighborhood that's less wealthy may be more supportive. You'll find more people in your community who don't measure by wealth or, more accurately, by spending. Remember what we said at the beginning—your value is not how much money you have, make, or spend! Your value is in who you are. Having like-minded people around you is better than owning the biggest house in town, or even living next door to it.

If you're in a city with relatively affordable housing, you can start calculating the cost of your commute. If you can get there by public transportation, that should be a relatively easy number to figure out. Even better if your employer subsidizes the trip!

If you'll be commuting by car, a good way to estimate the costs is to start with the IRS mileage reimbursement. In 2020, it is currently

57.5 cents a mile. If your commute is 20 miles each way, that's $2.13 per day, or $11.50/week and $575 per year, assuming a 2 weeks vacation (International Revenue Agency [IRS], 2020).[8]

The IRS reimbursement is essentially gas and regular wear and tear. It doesn't include the cost of repairs or insurance, so make sure your total commute cost adds those in. Compare the cost of the suburban house, including gas or transit costs and time, with the house in the city to make sure you are making the most cost-effective decision.

○ Add awnings, shade trees, and ceiling fans

These additions will help cool your house down in the summer. You may want awnings over your doors in addition to your windows; however, depending on the direction your house faces, you may not need awnings on all your windows. Focus on the ones that catch most of the sun's heat during the day.

While doing your landscaping, think about how large the trees will grow and if you have the right soil for them. Also, think about how long it will take for them to reach full height! You may not have the time to wait for a slow-growing tree to protect your west-facing windows. Though the tree may not be huge at first, make sure it has room to grow away from the house, accounting for root space. A large tree can grow to be quite some distance from the house and still provide enough shade in the summer.

Earlier in the chapter, we mentioned using existing ceiling fans to cool off or heat up the room. If you don't have fans, consider installing them. You can leave your a/c set at a much higher temperature at night when you're cooled by a fan right above the bed.

○ Preventative maintenance

Once you've renovated or found your wonderful home, keep it that way. Keep the paint fresh so water doesn't start seeping **197** into the house through cracks, and if your climate is friendly to mold and mildew, make sure you tend to susceptible areas regularly. Live in a dry climate? Use a humidifier.

Always repair foundation cracks. Clear out your gutters and downspouts, and angle the downspouts away from your basement and foundation. If you take care of the small issues, they won't snowball into bigger ones or reduce the efficiency you worked so hard to create.

Chapter Summary

SAVE MONEY AND SPEND WISELY

- Your home is a big-ticket item, and there are a number of ways to reduce the costs associated with it, though they may at first appear to be fixed.
- You can shop for better insurance rates, adjust your thermostat, and refinance your mortgage all immediately.
- In the medium term, consider renting out a room, replacing older appliance models for energy-efficient new ones, planning big furniture buys, and reusing and recycling things you already own.
- In the long term, consider whether your living arrangement is the best and most economical option for you at this time, and see what will be the best investment for you should you decide to move.
- When deciding to move, consider the neighborhood and whether it will fit your lifestyle.

In the next chapter, we will be discussing how to reduce your spending on electronics and devices.

---

[6] https://www.directenergy.com/blog/how-much-can-you-save-by-adjusting-your-thermostat/

[7] https://www.cnet.com/how-to/how-much-water-do-dishwashers-use/

[8] https://www.irs.gov/tax-professionals/standard-mileage-rates

Chapter FOUR

WIRED FOR SMART BUDGETING

IN the introduction, we talked about how some necessities of modern life, like cellphones and the internet, would have been unimaginable to your great-grandparents. Some of us tend to think of these as fixed costs too as a result, but they aren't.

Many of the devices themselves are similar; however, you may needlessly spend more money on one brand compared to another. There's absolutely no reason to stick with one brand out of loyalty or popularity. Save money by buying the device that will work just as well while costing you less because now is not the time to try to signal your belonging in a "club" and paying more than you need. The same goes for service providers.

There are plenty of ways to get what you want without overpaying, and you may not have been aware that they're out there. Therefore, I have rounded them up for you. Knowledge is power! So, go forth and save with this information.

Quick Tips to Start Now

As with most of the suggestions in this book, having to sit at home during the coronavirus means it's a great time to start implementing the following tips. You will get to be productive when you implement these changes, especially if you aren't working during this time.

- **Call for discounts on phone/Internet access**

  We mentioned this point briefly in the last chapter when discussing home and renter's insurance. Beyond material items, phone and Internet companies are even more notorious for dropping your monthly bill to keep you. You may want to jump on this fact as soon as possible when prices are so low too. Note that if you qualify for some kind of hardship assistance, you should absolutely take advantage of that too.

  It's much cheaper for them to keep you than to add a new customer, and the prices are essentially arbitrary anyway; it doesn't cost them $75 a month to keep the internet flowing into your Wi-Fi. Call and let them know you're ready to walk unless they can give you a better price.

  All service providers offer teaser rates for new clients, so it's not an empty threat on your part. This is true for most people, unless you live in a remote area with only one provider. In that case, you should still call and see if they can drop your rates. What's the worst that could happen? They'll say no. Nothing ventured, nothing gained.

- **Get rid of excess services you don't need on your cell phone, like call waiting**

  Many people barely use their phones for its original design, which was voice communication. If that's you, you definitely 201 don't need any extra voice services. Along with that, drop anything else you don't need from your plan.

- **Drop the landline if you have one**

  Now that cell phones have become pretty popular, you probably no longer need a landline. Your phone has GPS, so emergency services can still locate you quickly. Also, if you have an accident in your home, it's more likely that your mobile phone is closer to you than your landline anyway. At this point, for the vast majority of people, a landline is a completely unnecessary expense, so let it go.

- **Mobile phone alternatives**

  Once you've called your phone company and threatened to leave if you didn't get a lower rate, that's the best you can do, right?

  Wrong! At least for many.

  Most monthly service plans cost a certain amount depending on how much you think you'll use your data. If you use less than that, you've probably lost a lot of money. Likewise, if you use more, you may pay a surcharge or see your data throttled (slowed down).

  When considering one of the following alternatives, evaluate what your past usage has been for data—this includes streaming, checking your email, social media apps online, among other activities. Depending on your plan, that may or may not include text messaging. Check your past statements to see how much you normally use.

  Prepaid plans are often significantly cheaper than monthly service plans from the big carriers, at least when it comes to voice services. If you're a heavy data user, these plans may not work as well because they usually don't offer as many minutes on their data plans.

Another option for users who don't gobble up gobs of data is a pay-per-use service, such as Google Fi. You would only pay for the services you use, so if you don't use much data, you'll typically pay significantly less with these services.

You could also try Voice-Over-Internet-Protocol or VOIP. It's a cheaper way to talk, and it might even be a cheaper way to text! However, you won't be able to use it to watch your favorite videos or check your emails.[9]

o **Ditch cable TV and/or satellite TV**

With all the entertainment available on streaming services, there's no real reason to keep paying as much as you do on cable or satellite TV. You can probably get everything you want over the Internet, in one form or another.

In the next section, we'll be discussing streaming in more detail. For now, just cancel it. There are plenty of cheaper ways to access entertainment. I personally haven't had cable TV for over ten years. Whenever I visit my friends or relatives and there's a TV on, I constantly notice how much I save and that I'm not missing out!

I am not allowing that stream of mostly terrible films, bad news, and advertisements to attack and influence me. That stream was prepared by somebody who does not have the same values as I do, and their only purpose is to get watchers to sit through the ads. Why should I pay for something that I don't actually want?

Medium-Term to Implement in the Next Few Months

You've canceled your cable and gained a better deal on your phone and Internet services. There are a couple more steps you can take to help you save on these services in the next few months.

- **Avoid annual phone upgrades**

    Every year, each phone company unveils their latest device with a big advertising campaign and makes it seem like it's necessary, even though it's really not. Once in a while, a manufacturer might genuinely come out with a game changer in the new version that makes upgrading worth your while. Most of the time, however, there's hardly any difference between last year's version and this year's.

    Manufacturers often want to drain as much money out of your wallet as possible, and that does not mean you have to let them. An extra pixel on the camera, or a camera in a slightly different place or with a slightly sharper bevel won't actually change your life. Save your money.

    Having said that, these devices are designed for obsolescence. After a few years, your phone may stop working and you'll need to replace it. Be smart and purchase only what you need. Right now, I'm using a seven-year-old iPhone 5, which required a replacement for the broken display, as well as the battery three times. Some newer applications that just came out can no longer be installed on it; however it still works for emails, internet, and weather forecasts, which are all that I really use. I'm quite sure it will stop working within the next year. That will be when I choose a model that meets my requirements at that time.

o Consider the streaming services you need

Did you cut the cable cord easily because you're signed up for a whole bunch of streaming services? You probably don't need them all, and once you really think about it, you may realize you only need one or two. You may even realize you don't need any of them. You can probably get most of what you want on a free video platform like YouTube or Vimeo, so you can try checking those out first.

Keep in mind that you don't need to watch the same shows that everyone else in your office is watching. Back in the day, when there were only three channels, everyone talked about what was on TV because nearly everyone watched the same stuff. There wasn't much variety. Now, however, with the explosion of cable, streaming, and even user content, everyone watches something different, and everyone's conversations completely vary in terms of television.

If you have kids, it may make going streaming-free a bit harder. Although we can probably agree that kids shouldn't be spending as much time in front of a screen, it can really help if you work from home and need to distract them. If you are considering this change and want to start working remotely, you can find many more great tips in my book *Work from Home During and After the Economic Crisis*.

Kid-friendly shows are great life-savers in this regard. Likewise, if you don't have kids, think hard about whether you really need that kid's channel. They can be quite expensive. Focus your streaming and television watching on your personal interests.

Absolutely cannot give up streaming TV? You can first try giving it up for a month or two before declaring that is the case.   205

You might surprise yourself. If it is the case and you really *do* need some streaming services, then pick one that has the content you watch the most.

Long-Term Planning

There is only one major suggestion for the long term, and it's a pretty important one.

Stop spending so much time on your devices. Period. Substitute it with human contact, whether it's in-person or on the phone talking, and avoid texting or bantering on social media. Although spending time on social media seems to be the newest form of social communication, studies have found that it can actually make you feel more depressed, isolated, and less connected to others (Alyssa, n.d.).[10] Although social media most definitely has its uses and can help you connect with others, including for job-searching, so you might not want to give it up completely. Be judicious as you use it.

As shocking as it may sound, social media is the largest addiction people experience today. The apps are designed to give you a dopamine hit when you scroll over a nice image, see a message from a friend, or get a like. As with any addiction, those good feelings end quickly, so you continue scrolling to get another hit.

The apps and platforms were deliberately designed to be addictive, allowing the advertisers to show you their ads for a longer period while you scroll through your feed (Price, 2018).[11]

Social media uses your data and Wi-Fi, and the less data you're using on your devices, the cheaper your bills will be. There's no reason to pay through the nose for unlimited data when you can drop your usage significantly by lessening your time on social media. You will also end up feeling better as a result!

Chapter Summary

- While phones and Internet access are necessary for modern life, you don't have to overpay for them.
- Social distancing at home makes now a great opportunity to call for reducing monthly fees, and also to consider using a different type of service if doing so will lower your bills.
- Over the next few months, avoid needless device replacement and consider how many streaming services you really need.
- Reduce the amount of time you spend on your devices, as doing so will drop your data costs and help you reconnect.
- If you can after the pandemic, opt for in-person social connection, which will save you money and stronger social connections. Charge yourself with real social connection.

In the next chapter, we will learn all about cheap or free entertainment options that serve both your body and mind.

9 https://www.genvoice.net/can-people-send-and-receive-text-messages-via-voip/

10 https://www.bhpalmbeach.com/are-depression-and-social-media-usage-linked/

11 https://www.sciencefocus.com/future-technology/trapped-the-secret-ways-social-media-is-built-to-be-addictive-and-what-you-can-do-to-fight-back/

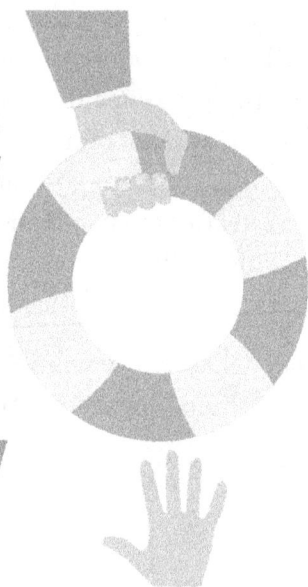

SAVE
MONEY
AND
SPEND
WISELY

Chapter FIVE

ENTERTAINMENT
THAT'S FUN AND FRUGAL

MOST of us are used to spending money on entertainment. We rent out or watch movies at the movie theater, buying buckets of popcorn, soda, and candy, along with the ticket for the film itself. We buy tickets to watch professional sports or for music concerts. Some of us have been known to use shopping as entertainment, heading to the mall to look at the stores, buy things we don't need, and eat food that isn't that nourishing. At the end of the day, many of us slump into the recliner, pick up the remote, and start flipping through channels.

We've paid one way or another for our entertainment in terms of money. Depending on your hobbies and what you enjoy watching passively, you might have paid hundreds or thousands of dollars for the privilege of inhaling what someone else has made.

Now, while you can't watch sports, go to the movies, or wander the mall aimlessly due to the pandemic restrictions, it is a terrific time to get yourself out of bad habits. You can still have plenty of fun without spending so much money. For now, we suddenly have a chance to break some habits! Replace passive activities with ones we genuinely enjoy and don't have to spend much, if any, money on.

Ready to start having an awesome time, even when staying at home? Then read on!

Quick Tips to Start Now

We have a good long list of things you can do right now while social distancing at home. Start with these suggestions, and you'll be surprised with how fast the days actually go by.

o **Go outside**

This one is pretty self-explanatory. Watching TV online or through streaming and spending time on your phone are passive activities that you would usually do sitting down. However, it turns out sitting all day is actually dangerous to your health! ("Dangers of Sitting," n.d.)[12]

Some people get confused by the shelter-in-place orders that many of us are currently living under. That doesn't mean you have to stay inside all day and never leave the house. You can definitely go out for walks, just make sure to practice social distancing and not get too close to others who might be out enjoying the sunshine with you. However, authorities in some countries have restricted going outside and to public places, which must be obeyed.

If you have a yard, get out there with your family and pet and play around. Kids don't do well cooped up indoors, and fresh air is good for everyone. Being out in nature is a boost for both your mental and physical health.

I personally like working in my garden. I plant various vegetables and fruits and care for my fruit bushes. Do I save a lot of money with this? Maybe not. However, I do get to enjoy eating my own products, fresh from the garden. I find they have the best taste. I also have flowers, trees, and a lot of plants around the house. I could remove these beauties and have just grass to mow, but I enjoy the sun and being out in the fresh air. Plus, I don't have to worry about going to the gym because gardening will give me a good amount of exercise.

Being outside also means you're getting away from your screens. If you absolutely must bring your phone with you, don't carry it in your hand. Put it in a pocket or purse. Also, remember to pay attention to what's going on around you. What's your child or spouse saying to you? What does the sky look like? Anything new in the neighborhood? Recognizing the answers to these questions will help keep you and your loved ones safe.

o **Skype/Zoom/FaceTime friends and family**

For most of us, being with our loved ones and close friends is not a possibility right now. Some of us have family living an entire country or more away. As discussed in the last chapter, using social media and texting may not work for everyone.

We humans are uniquely attuned to faces, and so it's important for us to be able to see the faces of the people we're talking to (Nottingham, 2017).[13] Therefore, when we can't be with each other physically, it's important to be able to see each other when possible. Phone calls are better than texting and typing; however, being face-to-face, even if we're not geographically close to one another, is best.

o **Learn an interesting new craft or skill online**

Fortunately, many of us have the Internet while we're all

staying home, which means, as long as you're using it correctly, you have a wealth of information at your fingertips.

It's easy to start scrolling and eventually end up down a rabbit hole! However, if you confine your search to something you're interested in while avoiding social media, you'll be OK. You may end up learning far more about your chosen subject than you thought you would.

Almost every hobby or craft that you can try is available online in the form of diagrams, blog posts, and even how-to videos. There are also discussion forums, tips and tricks articles, and "if only I'd known..." advice. A huge bonus to searching these up is that most of them are free!

No one can see you mess up or look goofy when you're in the comfort of your own home, so it's the perfect time to start learning something new. Who knows—you may have picked up a new and useful skill by the time social distancing is over.

o **Read/listen to books from the library**

Readers often like to buy books, but that can certainly get expensive. Investing in a library card would be a great option for these people because it's always free. Many local libraries are part of a larger system—for example, many US counties operate several libraries. If the one closest to you doesn't have the book you want, you can probably order it from another library in the system. Transfers are usually free too. If you don't already have a library card from your local library, you may be able to sign up online.

There are plenty of books available for reading. Some people prefer to listen, and you can download audiobooks from various sources, often for free. You may be able to download free ebooks from your library as well. Plus, just as with audiobooks, there are a number of sources that are either free or reasonably cheap. 213

Novels help you empathize with other people by allowing you to step into the minds of the characters. If you're having trouble understanding why other people are having such a hard time with isolation, reading a novel may be a great idea for you!

There is a lot of information on the Internet, but the vast majority of it is in bite-size pieces. That information is also often redundant from post to post. Books, however, can provide a much deeper dive into the subject you're interested in.

- **No browsing or putting items in your online cart - buy nothing**

Break the habit of online shopping. As of the writing of this book (March 2020), the major product shippers are sending out priority items such as cleaning supplies first. In other words, now is an excellent time to practice not shopping. If you don't need anything, stop browsing.

It can be easy to get mesmerized by the advertising in front of you on the screen. Remember—these platforms are designed to capture you so the advertisers can get their content in front of you. Admen and women have been in the game of influencing you for decades, and the easiest way to avoid losing the game is to refuse to play it in the first place.

Don't bother with deal sites either, unless you need something specific. Disable the notifications or unsubscribe from their emails, as the only thing you will miss out on is having your wallet drained.

Challenge yourself to buy nothing except for the necessities like groceries and cleaning supplies for a few months. If you run out of something and need to replace it, you can do that. However, you should check whether you really need to replace it before you do.

o **If you must add to your cart, don't click "buy" right away**

Sometimes, old habits die hard. Before you go online shopping, however, disable one-click or anything else that makes buying online instant. You want it to be hard and forcing you to think about it because, the more rational you are about it, the less you'll actually purchase.

If you do put something in the cart, leave it for a few hours. Advertisements telling you to come back and buy will pop up automatically due to the site's algorithms, but you need to resist. You might see a price pop up that claims you'll only get the special price if you buy now.

Marketers aim for your emotions. They play on your fear of losing a special discount or missing something important if you don't buy now because they know that, if you take the time to consider whether you need a product, you probably won't buy it. Thus, you are faced with the "buy now with a discount" techniques. Remember—they don't care about you and don't have your best interests in mind. They have their own profit motive in mind, which may or may not align with your values. Most of the time, it doesn't.

No one on the other side of the screen is desperate for you to buy! There's an automated algorithm that has been programmed to ask you these questions before you leave the site. The algorithm analyzes your behavior and uses cookies on your computer to discover a lot about you. It then directs the conversation specifically to people similar to you: women, young adults, or people living in certain regions. Advertisers know precise questions increase the purchase rate, so don't let them game you.

Likewise, consider buying from Chinese companies such as Aliexpress or Wish. The price is usually a fraction compared to the US stores online and, depending on the product, you could 215 find the same items 60-90% cheaper. Many US stores may sell exactly the same product, but nicely packed and with a brand attached. Despite the cheaper cost, delivery time may be longer, and it can take weeks due to shipment time from China, custom clearance, and transfer between several shippers. Therefore, make note that just because it only costs $1 doesn't mean you have to buy it instantly. Add in the cost of shipping—US online companies may also offer free delivery and discounts for Black Friday or Cyber Monday. Be wise and compare product pricing overall.

Medium-Term to Implement in the Next Few Months

Once things have calmed down—whatever that may look like—there will be time and opportunity to get together with friends and family. That means sharing and connecting, which are both important to human beings.

Rather than watching TV or sports, try joining a recreational sports league, going for a walk, or hanging out with your friends. Such will satisfy the human need for connection, along with your body's need for activity to stave off inflammatory diseases like cardiovascular disease, Type II diabetes, and certain cancers. It also protects your brain from neurodegenerative diseases, such as Alzheimer's and dementia.

- **Hang out with friends at the local park or each other's houses instead of hitting the bars**

  You might be hanging out with your friends over Skype right now, but that will probably change at some point. Don't stop being with friends now that you can be geographically close to them!

  Going to the bar with friends does allow you to stay connected; however, it also allows you to spend a lot of money that you don't need to spend and doesn't provide you with much mental or physical stimulation.

Try to do two things at once when making time with your friends, if you can. For example, you can go to the park with your friends, effectively satisfying your needs for human connection and for nature at the same time. It's hard to sit still on a beautiful day, so you may as well get some movement in as well.

Rather than going to the bar having overpriced drinks, go to your house or your friend's house with your own drinks. Doing so will save you a ton of money. Play games, have fun, and exercise your brain a little.

o Become an artist

There's no reason that you always have to read someone else's story, watch their movie, or listen to their music. You can try picking up the instrument that you played as a kid. You may have lost the ability to read music by this point, but that's what online tutorials are for!

Many people experience the deep human need to create. Why are you watching someone else's show? Write your own story, make your own movie, and film yourself doing a silly dance or creating something interesting. There's no reason you have to settle for someone else's when making your own is great for your brain (Stahl, 2018).[14]

When you get together with people with whom you share common interests, you'll also be connecting and socializing. Just like with close friends, all this art making and befriending can take place at someone's house or the park; therefore, there is no need to rent out a pricey studio or go to a fancy bar. After joining a community with people who share your interests, you will often receive great understanding, support, and encouragement from them.

- **Potluck dinners with friends and colleagues**

  Some people really enjoy eating different foods while not cleaning up after themselves after every meal! However, going out to eat constantly can become pretty expensive. Even if you only venture to a cafe or bistro—both of which tend to be cheaper than a fine dining restaurant—you're still spending money you don't really need to.

  Instead, you can agree to potluck at someone's house over a set number of times each week or month. Who brings what rotates between you, along with who hosts. You can create themes and work around food sensitivities, all the while eating great food that others have cooked. You may have to clean when it's your turn to host, but you will still be saving more money than if you went out to eat over the same frequency.

  Some people formalize this into a supper or dinner club. You can do that too, if you prefer the feel of a more luxurious treat. However, you can also stay with the coziness and informality of potluck. It's a great way to get to know people you work with on a deeper level, so, without formally networking, you will still be networking. It's also a great way to get to know your neighbors if you decide to start one in your neighborhood.

- **Amateur sports games instead of professional ones**

  If you really want to go watch some sports instead of playing them, consider your local leagues instead. Major pro sports tickets are incredibly expensive, and the games are held pretty far from home for many people; therefore, you also need to factor in the cost of getting there and back.

  Don't forget all the money you would probably spend on food and memorabilia at a pro sports arena. Many people feel the need to memorialize their trip with some kind of souvenir.

Thus, are you going to the game because you love the sport, the players, or do you love to spend money? If it's the sport, you could probably go watch the local teams play instead for far less money or for free. They're less likely to be selling expensive souvenirs, in addition to much cheaper tickets. The hot dog and soda is probably more reasonably priced than it is at the fancy stadium. In some cases, you might not even be hungry because you haven't had to make a day of it. The money you do spend at amateur games would also probably support the local club or kids learning the sport.

You're more likely to see friends and colleagues at a local game than across a crowded arena that seats thousands. When you really think about it, there are a lot of reasons to go watch local games in your area!

o Beyond just watching sports, go try them out yourself

To take the above argument even farther, if you really love the sport, you could also try playing it. Therefore, get out there on the field and give it your all. You can join a rec or amateur league in whatever sport you desire, and some sports—like swimming— have a Masters level for swimmers who are past college age, and you can join one of those teams. Your local YMCA or gym probably has some adult sports teams too. You can pick your level and have at it.

The main reason to join a team is not necessarily to be the best in the league, but to go out, have fun, and get a bit of exercise too. You can even see if your neighbors or colleagues want to play a sport with you. Many large companies support their employees organizing sports teams, games, or running together in the local race.

If you have injuries, you'll need to be careful. In most cases, you won't be alone, and you may still be able to find a sport or 219 league that caters to people who can't move as fast or throw as hard, depending on your injury. For example, you may be unable to play tackle football anymore, but flag football with close friends might be perfect for you. In addition, there are plenty of physical activities you can do at any age, like archery.

- **Go to the matinee if attending a symphony/the theater**

Most artistic institutions have both expensive and cheaper performances. No matter what it is, matinees are always cheaper and are usually held in the early afternoon. Theaters will often run performances from Friday to Sunday, and the least expensive ticket is the Sunday afternoon matinee, so grab it!

Movie theaters will often discount the early movie times—before noon—quite cheaply. Otherwise, they may have special days where tickets are cheaper, such as Tuesdays, when they don't often have a lot of attendees.

- **Go to free days at the museums and other attractions**

The vast majority of museums and other attractions have time during the week when entrance is free. In some lucky cases, entrance is free all the time, like the Smithsonian in Washington, DC or the zoo in St. Louis, MO. These attractions and the days they are free may not be as convenient, and they most likely won't be. Just as movie theaters pick Tuesday for their discount day because that's when people rarely go to the movies, these attractions will pick a time when they don't typically get many visitors. Depending on the size of the attraction and its location, you may be able to go several times in one month and see something different!

Not all museums are for children, even though many people think they are. Some are designed for children, so you should absolutely take your kids there, especially on the free days.

However, as an adult, you shouldn't be at all worried about going in just because of others' perceptions. Chances are, if there aren't any large museums nearby, there will be a small historical society or art museum that you can check out from time to time.

Otherwise, your community may have other attractions with free days. If you're not sure, check online or look up your local chamber of commerce for tourist information. Either one will let you know what's free and when.

o Go to the park

Most parks are free, though you may need a pass for certain national parks. Local parks often have picnic areas, basketball or tennis courts, and paths to hike. They're a great way to get active in the fresh air. Parks become even better when you visit them with friends.

o Look at discounts you qualify for at parks, movies, etc.

You may be affiliated with a company or an organization that provides discounts for attractions like amusement parks, movie theaters, and even live theater performances. Large companies often donate money to their communities as part of their philanthropic efforts, and you might be able to take advantage of that as an employee. Likewise, you might be part of an organization—AAA, for example—that provides its members with discounts to various places. Your credit card company may give you discounts as part of its rewards program, so go online to see what's available to you.

If you go to an attraction frequently, you could even consider a membership with them instead. Think about how many times you attended this place over the course of the year and how much the tickets are. If the cost turns out to be more than that of an annual membership, you should probably become a member. You'll often get some additional free perks as well.

However, only become a member after you've been there and know you'll go back. Don't be like the people who make a New Year's resolution and buy a gym membership, then never go again after January.

Long-Term Planning

By now, you should have a pretty long list of ideas that will keep you happy and occupied without having to spend a lot of money. There are more, too, when looking out toward the long term. How do you stay connected and entertained for little money when you're busy and earning money again? By then, the need to save may not feel quite so urgent.

Do what you enjoy and what feels good for you. By then, you'll have built up a habit of creativity and recycling or reusing instead of buying something new. For example, you may want to jam on instruments with your friends instead of merely listening to a playlist.

- **Join a group devoted to your hobby**

  While at home during the coronavirus pandemic, you're probably trying out a few new hobbies, such as an instrument or craft. In the early stages, you may not really know what you're doing and are a bit worried about making a fool of yourself.

  Once the awkwardness has passed, however, you'll then have some experience under your belt. Though you may not be the best one in your group if you join one, who really cares? Just have fun. Joining a group of people with similar interests is a great way to connect when trying to improve or complete a new project.

You can find groups by looking through sites such as Meetup or Eventbrite online, and you can even check a journal or web forum on your craft. Go to physical meetings if you can because those will usually be better ways to get to know people. However, if the groups are all far away from you, online is better than no group at all.

These groups will be free most of the time, especially when online. If you can't find a free group but know of some like-minded people in your area, you can organize one yourself. You can meet at the park, a local coffee shop, or in your own home. You are the organizer, so you will get to choose what works best for you.

o Go to local festivals and events

Destination concerts and festivals have been popular since Woodstock in the 1960s. Now, depending on your taste in music and fests, you might be looking to hit a Renaissance Faire, Coachella, Stagecoach, or Electric Daisy Carnival, to name a few.

Most of these places are pretty pricey across the board, and you will probably have to buy pretty much everything there, including water, food, and souvenirs. There is also the general cost of the festival, none of which are cheap. Add in accommodation and travel costs, and you're looking at a huge expense.

Instead of planning a destination trip, scout around to see what's near you. If it's all about the music, there's probably a nearby spot hosting a festival. Maybe you only need a day pass. Many communities also have their own Renaissance festivals, concerts, and various holiday attractions. Save some money by going local.

- **Make your own activity**

If you're a bit more ambitious and you have friends who are into it, why not stage your own concert lineup? Check out venues around town that are friendly to local bands, and let all your friends know on social media. You can also create shareable invites for friends to send to their friends. Then, you and your buddies can all jam out together and have a lot of fun!

People like to see what's going on locally. Depending on how much work you want to do in advance, you might even get local businesses to sponsor. They get their names in front of your audience, and you receive some money to defray expenses.

Another option is to make your own weekend RenFest or holiday event. It probably won't be the next Coachella, but it will at least be fun.

- **Volunteer at interesting places/events**

One of the best ways to get into an event or place for free is to volunteer. If you love classical music but don't want to pay for the tickets, you can volunteer to usher. At the historical society, you could maybe sign up to be a guide, or you could be a tour guide at your favorite local museum. Love being around animals? Volunteer at your local animal shelter.

Whatever your interest is, you'll probably find plenty of opportunities to volunteer. They'll normally provide you with some training, so don't worry about not being an expert when you start. Also, when you're volunteering, you're at the service of other people, which can make the brain pretty happy.

Chapter Summary

o You don't have to spend a lot of money—or any money at all—to entertain yourself once you get creative with how you want to spend your time.

o Now is the perfect time to break yourself from spending and mindless browsing habits and learn something new because you can do so in private.

o Once the restrictions have been lifted, you can hang out with your friends for free or cheap by joining recreational teams. Doing so allows you to play the sports you enjoy watching.

o After a while and once you've learned your new skill, you can be more confident in joining groups devoted to it and even consider making your own local festival or concert.

o By saving money on entertainment and getting creative about how you have fun, you're also improving your health both mentally and physically.

In the next chapter, we will go over how to reduce the costs of owning and renting vehicles.

---

[12] https://www.betterhealth.vic.gov.au/health/healthyliving/the-dangers-of-sitting

[13] https://wistia.com/learn/marketing/power-of-faces-in-video

[14] https://www.forbes.com/sites/ashleystahl/2018/07/25/heres-how-creativity-actually-improves-your-health/#18d6ba0913a6

SAVE
MONEY
AND
SPEND
WISELY

Chapter **SIX**

REVISIT YOUR VEHICLES

IN a car-centric country, it's easy to assume that every person of driving age needs at least one car; in some cases, they may prefer a motorcycle or a boat. Due to what appears to be cheap leases, many drivers trade up to a new vehicle every couple of years when the lease is up. Unfortunately, every vehicle—with the exception of vintage ones—is a depreciating asset, thus the value of the car dives the instant you roll it off the lot.

When reconsidering your spending plan, take a look at your fleet and see if there's anything you want to change. We have some tips for reducing various costs on your vehicles too, but getting rid of a vehicle you don't need will be the biggest moneysaver.

Quick Tips to Start Now

There are a few things that you can do right now that don't require a lot of thought. Nevertheless, they will still save you money.

- **Vehicle you don't need, like a boat? Sell it.**

  There's a saying that the two best days for a boat owner are the day they buy it and the day they sell it. Most boats are money sinks, as they require a lot of maintenance and storage space if you don't live in an area where you can leave it in the water year-round.

  If you spend a lot of time on or live in it, you may not want to sell it. However, if you rarely get a chance to sail it, even during the perfect season, you should consider selling it. You may not get back what you put into it, but it will give you some money back. On the bright side, you can then avoid maintenance and storage costs.

  Love boats? You can still rent one, as most marinas have a boat rental program.

  If it's not a boat, you may have a motorcycle or other vehicle you don't use often. Though bikes don't require as much maintenance, if you rarely ride it, it could be worth selling.

- **Shop insurance**

  If you didn't already bundle your home and car together when you reviewed the suggestions in the home chapter, you can do it now. There are a lot of insurance companies out there, so if you threaten to leave about your car insurance this time, it'll be credible.

  The company knows you have options. Just like all the mobile phone services, insurance companies find it much easier and cheaper to hang on to their current customers and would rather drop the price a bit for you than spend the money to replace you as a customer. Also, don't forget that, even if you lease a car, you're still required to maintain insurance on it.

229

Note that older cars aren't really worth that much due to depreciation. It doesn't stop the minute you roll off the lot, but continues throughout the life of your car. Collision coverage replaces or repairs your car if you're at fault in an accident, and comprehensive covers things like vandalism, theft, and animal collisions. If you have an older car, reduce your costs by dropping collision and comprehensive coverage. Don't ever drop your liability!

Once your car is at the point where you wouldn't make a major repair—like replacing the transmission—or 10% of the premium is more than you'd receive for a payout, you should consider selling it for parts. Wear the car out, then use the money you saved from no longer paying those premiums to get a new one.

o Defensive (and inexpensive) driving

There is a saying "to drive like one's grandma," and although it may annoy some readers to hear, driving "like your grandma" will actually really help with your gas mileage and reduce the overall cost of your gas. These tips are also good for defensive driving, so you'll be able to avoid more accidents too.

Stay a reasonable distance behind the car in front of you by obeying the 3-second rule, which will help you avoid sudden accidents. Count three seconds from a stationary item (like a light pole) when the car ahead of you passes by. If you pass it before you finish counting, you're probably too close, so drop back slightly. The faster you go, the more distance you need between you and that car. Slamming on the brakes, stomping on the gas, and speeding are all bad for your gas mileage. It depends on the car, but the miles per gallon (MPG) starts decreasing around 50 miles per hour in many vehicles (US Department of Energy [USDE], 2013).[15] In addition to avoiding unnecessary gas and break use, do your best to avoid weaving in and out of traffic and cutting people off. Doing so is rude and terrible on your gas mileage.

230

If applicable, take out/off excess weight and your roof rack. The rack reduces the aerodynamics of your car, and having too much in your car can also decrease your gas mileage. Reducing the amount you carry also makes you less of a target for thieves because there will be nothing for them to steal.

Idling uses a lot of gas, especially if you have the a/c on, so you're better off turning the car off instead.

When you're on the highway, use cruise control. The car's computer is much more accurate than you are at determining how much power you need to stay at a given speed. Plus, on a long car trip, you can stretch your legs a bit while driving when cruise is set.

o Shop around for good gas prices

There are apps you can download that will tell you the prices of every gas station within the vicinity. With these apps, you can plan ahead. Rather than driving around on an empty fuel tank and desperate for a gas station, leave a little in the tank and look for a better price. Gas stations near freeways are notorious for higher prices, compared to others further away.

In some places, you can get a better price by paying in cash or using debit instead of credit. If you live somewhere where those options are accepted, make sure you have enough cash for gas at the end of the week. Some gas companies also offer discounts or perks if you use their credit card to buy gas. As always, if you pay by credit, pay it off at the end of the month so they can't use compounding interest against you.

Some grocery stores offer points off on gas when you buy a certain amount in the store. If you normally shop in one place, this might be a good deal for you.

o Keep tires inflated & use the right oil

Gas mileage decreases when your tires aren't fully inflated, and it's also much safer to drive on properly inflated tires! You may 231 be able to see if they're flat, but it's best to also check the tire pressure before you drive and when the tires are cold. The tires warm up as they roll, which will inflate the pressure reading. Inflate to the manufacturer's guidelines.

The manufacturer should have also specified the right oil to use with the car. You may find a cheaper oil; however, if it's not up to spec, it may cause damage in the long term. If you have someone change the oil, make sure they're using the right formula. Likewise, you don't necessarily have to change the oil every 3,000 miles. That was the old standard, but most cars can roll perfectly fine up to 10,000 miles or even 20,000 miles. Lease contracts may also require regular maintenance.

- **No driving is the cheapest way to drive**

  Needless to say, less driving also means less overall mileage and wear and tear on your car. We don't have a lot of public transportation here in the US, so most of us do have to drive. However, you can drive less by combining errands together, rather than making multiple trips. Not only are you saving money in terms of mileage, but you would also be saving time.

Medium-Term to Implement in the Next Few Months

Some of the following steps may take a little bit more planning or computing of costs, so that you can weigh advantages and disadvantages more accurately.

- **If you have more than one car, decide if you really need all of them**

  Two adults in a household means you need two cars, right? Well, not necessarily. Here's where you really have to spend some time thinking about it. If both of you work in opposite directions from each other, have different work schedules, and

SAVE MONEY AND SPEND WISELY DURING AND AFTER THE ECONOMIC CRISIS **CHAPTER SIX**

without public transportation in your area, you may need to keep both. But, what if that's not the case?

If there is a lot of public transportation near you and the places you frequent, you can probably get away with one car. This is the same as if you lived and worked near someone you could carpool with. Many families in the United States have been able to get away with having just one car, and you can too.

o **Decide if it may be cheaper to keep a second car or use a taxi/ridesharing service.**

Recall that the cost of a car isn't just the upfront cost—it includes maintenance, insurance, repairs, and gas too. Even if you don't drive a single mile all year, you'll still spend hundreds on insurance, fees, and maintenance. Thus, if one of you doesn't really drive that much, do you really need that second car? Can you get by calling the occasional cab or rideshare? While someone else is driving, you can read, prep for a meeting, or just chat with the driver and enjoy the drive.

You can also consider using a rental car service, such as Zipcar, and seeing if that can save you money. We live in an era of options and not everyone needs to own or lease a car to get around. Explore some of these other choices and see if they'd work for you, and you will also help reduce traffic associated with environmental impact.

o **Perform preventative maintenance**

The best way to keep your car going for a long time is to make sure it receives preventative maintenance. Most cars have a schedule for major services: a comprehensive service at 90,000 miles, timing belt replacement (for cars that still have them), oil changes, and filter replacements.

233

Not getting these things done on a timely basis means a shorter life for your car. It may be money out of your pocket when you bring it to a mechanic, but it's a short-term cost that will benefit you in the long run.

o **DIY the repairs and service that you can**

Granted, many of today's cars run on computers instead of the mechanical devices as old cars did. However, you can still look up the meanings of the various lights and icons that appear on your dashboard. Doing so can help you figure out car repairs yourself, rather than going to visit a mechanic.

You may not have a jack to pick your car up for tire rotation maintenance; however, you should be able to at least change the oil yourself. You can also replace the windshield wipers, inflate the tires, among other repairs.

If you're a relatively handy person, you could probably do even more—changing out the cabin or other air filters, replacing light bulbs, battery, or sundry other small parts. As with all crafts and hobbies, there are tutorials online for practically everything! Note that not all repairs should be done at home, however, and some should only be tackled by professionals.

o **Carpool when you can**

Carpooling also allows you to do two things at once, and you will get to know people better. If you and a friend, neighbor, or colleague work in the same place or at least somewhat close to each other, carpooling works really well. You'll have some companions for the ride, which is helpful when there's a lot of traffic or a long distance. If you're not the one driving, you could probably catch up on some calls, emails, or other work-related tasks. It's also less wear and tear on everyone's vehicles because the frequency at which you drive would be less.

It may also help if you live in an area with high-occupancy vehicle (HOV) lanes, which are faster. The residents in an outer suburb of Virginia started "slugging" in one of the commuter lots. Within this transaction, people who wanted a ride would line up, and single drivers would pick up a passenger or two, thus allowing the car to drive in the HOV lane. Most office space in the area may be clustered in one spot, and it has decent public transportation for a US city. Therefore, once the car entered the main city, everyone was pretty close to their destination. This transaction would be the same coming back to the commuter lot.

Long-term planning

You might have learned some new things in the past couple of sections, but now it's time to ask the big questions. Why are you driving your specific vehicle, and should you make a switch? If you live far from where you work, should you consider making a change? Think about a different lifestyle if you're the type who leases cars.

o **Is your vehicle suited to your life? If not, trade it in.**

Very few people have large families, haul or tow cargo regularly, or drive often into the hinterlands and off-road. Many drivers spend most of their driving time going from home to work, the mall, or a grocery store—all on paved roads.

Pickup trucks are usually necessary in only one of two instances: when moving heavy loads or cargo, or when driving somewhere that requires a high clearance factor, such as unpaved or rocky roads. Otherwise, pickup trucks are more of a *want* rather than a *need*.

Sport utility vehicles (SUVs) aren't really necessary unless you have a large family. They can also be quite dangerous to pedestrians and young drivers, as they can be a little more difficult to control. **235**

The best car for most drivers are those that are small and fuel-efficient. They may not appear as cool on the surface, but they will save you a lot of money. Similar to boats, not only is a big car longer, but also wider and taller. All it requires are extra material and different construction. In other words, you will overpay larger vehicles twice—upfront when you buy it and during its life—for higher consumption and regular expenses.

Electric cars are great for gas mileage, but the infrastructure for electric cars is spotty. One city may have excellent facilities for electric vehicles, whereas another an hour away may have nothing. In that case, a hybrid may be a better option. You can choose a plug-in hybrid, though it may be better if you have a house or garage where you can plug it in overnight. Otherwise, you can choose an old-school hybrid that charges its battery through braking. Even a small, non-hybrid car will be more fuel-efficient than a large car. Having a smaller car will also limit how much you can put in it, increasing your gas mileage.

o **Buy used**

A new car doesn't really have to be brand-new, just new to you. You can let someone else handle the cost of the depreciation.

Make sure it's a good value, though. Pull the reports using its vehicle identification Number (VIN) to see if it's been in any accidents that might cause long-term damage. You'll want to know if it was previously a rental car or fleet vehicle, as cars with these histories were usually not taken care of well, neither by the owners nor the users. The fastest car will have been a company car.

You can consider asking a mechanic friend to check it out. Another option is to buy a certified "preowned" vehicle from a dealership. They normally come with a warranty that can protect the car even further.

o **Consider moving to a place that's closer to work, or one that has better public transportation.**

If you live far from work and commute every day, it isn't just about the wear and tear on your car, but that on you and your family too. In my book *Work from Home During and After the Economic Crisis*, I describe trending remote job opportunities for freelancers and entrepreneurs from home. 46% of freelancers chose to work remotely because of personal circumstances, such as caring for children or other relatives, or if they have health limitations and disabilities (Upwork, 2020).[16]

Perhaps you moved out to a suburb because the house had a yard and single bedrooms for the kids. However, you may never have time to spend with the kids because you're gone before they go to school in the morning, and you don't come back until it's dark. Is a long commute the best use of your time? What if you moved to a smaller house that was closer? In that case, you could eat breakfast with the kids and maybe have time to play with them before it gets dark. It won't kill the kids to share bedrooms.

Don't have kids? You could still use the extra time to yourself or with your partner if you have one.

There are other cases that this advice would alleviate, such as bad traffic during your commute or if your kids need to be supervised when playing outside in your specific environment. You could also consider living where there's good public transportation. Such communities tend to be walkable and have more of a "togetherness" feel.

o **Stop leasing cars every couple of years**

If you lease cars, you are spending too much money without benefiting from an asset. Again, think wants and needs—no one needs a new car every two years. If you like variety, pick **237** something that's cheaper to change out every few years, like the upholstery on your chairs or the paint on the walls.

Ending a lease early can be very expensive, so you may need to wait until the end of the term if you decide to stop leasing. At the end, you can trade in for another lease, turn it in, then walk away or buy the car you've been leasing. If you buy that car, you're probably spending too much (Swartz, 2020).[17] You might owe some fees in the end, especially if there was excessive wear and tear. Make sure you give them back everything the car came with (mats, key fobs, etc.)

Cars on the road today can go well over 100 thousand miles, thus the cost you pay to buy them amortizes itself over the years. I once bought a 2004 Mazda Miata new for about $26,000 and drove it for 13 years until the head gasket blew. At that point, it wasn't worth the repair cost, so I bought a used car to replace it.

The $26K over 13 years can calculate to $2,000 a year. In other words, the cost amortized to less than $170/month over the life of the car, which is a lot less than what a lease goes for these days! I'd taken out a 5-year loan to pay for it, and, once it was paid off, I had no car payment. Think about having a car payment of $0 for 8 years—it's pretty sweet! You can also save up the amount of that car payment and be ready to go for a new-to-you car in cash once you've driven the old one into the ground.

Chapter Summary

- Not everyone needs to own a car, and some people may have other vehicles they don't use enough to justify the costs of maintenance and repair.
- Drivers can sell vehicles they don't need immediately and reduce gas costs by making adjustments to how they drive and the cargo they carry.
- In one to three months, consider selling off a second car if you can get by without it through carpooling, rideshare, taxis, or transit, and doing as much DIY servicing and repair as you can to your current car.
- Over the long term, think about the kind of vehicle your household truly needs, and replace it when necessary with a used vehicle instead of a brand new one.

In the next chapter, we'll discuss how to reduce your clothing costs, even if you must wear business dress to work.

---

[15] https://afdc.energy.gov/files/u/publication/gas-saving_tips_july_2013.pdf

[16] https://www.upwork.com/press/2019/10/03/freelancing-in-america-2019/

[17] https://www.policygenius.com/loans/what-happens-at-the-end-of-a-car-lease/

SAVE
MONEY
AND
SPEND
WISELY

Chapter SEVEN

DRESS TO IMPRESS (YOUR WALLET)

CLOTHING is definitely necessary; however, you don't have to buy designer clothes. You also don't have to purchase "fast fashion" that is bad for both the environment and workers who make it. You might be thinking that it's impossible to dress well on a budget or without resorting to cheap clothing designed to fall apart after a few spins in the washing machine. The reality is that it actually isn't, and this book contains some tips on maintaining your current wardrobe, so you won't have to constantly replenish it.

Quick Tips to Start Now

We've got tips on what you can do right now during social distancing. These tips may even give you something interesting to do while you can't go out and shop.

○ **Implement a buy-nothing plan**

This has a very simple premise: commit to buying nothing, including shopping online. Most of us have too many clothes and only wear a fraction of our wardrobe anyway.

You may need to replace items that wear out faster, such as underwear, but decide that you will not buy anything new for a set time. Try for at least six months, if not a year. That decision will carry you through the months until the stores open back up. Avoid the temptation.

○ **Sell clothes you don't need if possible and take designer items to consignment**

Do you have anything you never wear? Maybe it's too small, big, or it makes you feel older. If any of your clothes have stains that won't come out, toss or cut them up for rags. No one will accept stained clothes. In general, there's no point in holding on to any of these items.

Have designer items in good condition? You can try checking out consignment shops instead. Once the garment sells, the shop owner will give you a part of the proceeds. In this transaction, you may end up with more money than if you sold outright—that way, the owner won't have to come up with the cash.

You can also try auction sites online or resale shops if you want to sell any of your old clothes.

○ **Make small repairs where necessary so you can wear clothes again**

If you have clothes that need little repairs to be either wearable or sellable, now's the time. It will really benefit you if you spend some time working on them.

Sew on buttons, fix unraveled hems, and reinforce rips along the seams. If you're creative, you could even think of ways to repurpose the item into something different. Consider adding decorative trim or thread, changing out the buttons, and refreshing a tired wardrobe. You might end up with almost an entirely new wardrobe for close to nothing in the end!

- **Don't wash too often, and don't throw things in the dryer**

  Get in the habit of extending the life of your clothing. Washers and dryers, especially commercial ones in apartment buildings, tend to be extremely harsh on your clothes. If you didn't get your clothing dirty when you wore it, you probably don't need to wash it. A better alternative for your clothes is hanging it up and letting it air out instead of throwing it straight in the laundry. Note that white shirts may be the exception, as they tend to discolor quickly around the armpits.

  Likewise, try to avoid using the dryer when you can. Many people need to dry their sheets, towels, and other household items; however, clothing can be hung up instead. You should especially consider this if you have an outdoor area where they can dry your clothes in the fresh air. If not, find a spot inside where your clothes can rest until they're dried.

  Not only does this tactic save money in the long term by making your wardrobe last longer. It also saves money because you won't be washing and drying as much, meaning fewer dollars into the commercial machines or lower water and electric bills, depending on where you do your laundry.

Medium-Term to Implement in the Next Few Months

Once social distancing orders have ended, you can probably try some wardrobe changes. How is that possible with a buy-nothing plan and not overspending? Once again, it's time to get creative!

o Clothing swaps with friends

These can be a lot of fun once we can gather together again. You can do this at someone's house or at your own—invite your friends over and have them bring clean clothing they're willing to trade. Consider also bringing your own drinks and make it a real party. You would still end the night with some new clothes—at least, new to you.

o Yard sales

Sometimes, your entire neighborhood may decide to have a yard sale. If they do, go up and down the street and check out what your neighbors have to offer. These events are particularly great for kids' clothes because there are usually older kids who want to sell old clothes they've outgrown. No matter the reason, some clothes will be perfect for your kids.

Yard sales work for finding household items and adult clothing too. You never know what you'll find! People may have been hiding clothes that don't fit them in the back of their closet, so you may even find clothes that have never been worn.

In some cases, people set up yard sales because they're moving or found they had too much stuff in their house. Check local listings and handmade signs that can direct you toward a house with sales. You can also have your own yard sale showcasing items you no longer need. You will not only earn some money, but you will also get to learn more about your neighbors while having a bit of fun.

o Browse without bringing your wallet

Are you one of those people who just enjoy shopping? Do you like to see what's out there or how others put outfits together? All of that is completely fine, and you might even get some great ideas for your own wardrobe!

The problem lies in your likeliness to actually shop when you browse. To avoid temptation, don't bring your wallet with you while shopping—leave it at home instead. You could also try locking it in the glove box of your car and parking far away from where you plan to window shop. Once you have your preventative measures in place, you can then browse to your heart's content, taking in various wardrobe ideas without worrying about spending money. If you see something you really like, by the time you leave, the desire will have worn off.

- **When buying, make sure the clothes don't need special care**

  Dry cleaning is expensive. The chemicals used are extremely toxic, and green cleaners may also be too expensive. When you're buying clothes you plan to wear often, avoid those with a "dry clean only" label because you will spend too much cleaning them.

  Instead, make sure it can go in the washer. Business suits tend to be dry-clean only, but you shouldn't have to clean them after every wearing. Some brands make suits that can be tossed in the laundry, so check for these options first.

- **Care for your clothes, so they can last longer**

  This is why you shouldn't buy dry-clean-only clothes: they'll wear out faster if you put them in the laundry! The more you can abide by the garment label, the longer your clothing will last, assuming you haven't been purchasing fast-fashion items that are designed to fall apart after one season. As a general rule, if you see a hole, mend it if you can.

  When you do need to do laundry, it's often helpful to turn the item inside out, as long as you don't have stains on the front. Doing so keeps your clothes looking new longer, as the washing machine agitation can be harsh.

You don't necessarily need fabric softener sheets, which are bad for the environment and can be expensive. You can use a laundry ball of foil, tennis ball, felted wool ball, or plastic hedgehog dryer ball to soften and prevent static cling.

Wash your woolen items carefully and reshape them to dry. You'll need to lay them flat in most cases. Use a laundry bag for delicates, so they don't wind around the agitator. Make sure to pretreat stains or try to dab them out immediately, so you don't have to give up on a garment just because you spilled something on it.

o Shop out of season

If you do need to replace items, try to shop out of season and when they're cheapest. Stores charge high prices at the beginning of the season, so expect to pay the price if you're looking for a new swimsuit just before summer. Thus, you can try buying at the end of the season. Though the variety won't be there, some good deals may be while stores make way for new merchandise.

o Buy on sale

Planning ahead helps prevent mindless spending. If you know you need a certain item, give yourself some time before you buy. Wait to see if you can find it on sale; that way, you're not forced to buy something at full price.

Try to use coupons too, if you have any. Using a store credit card often works and it may give you a discount; however, you must pay it off at the end of the month. Do not allow your clothing purchases to be used against you in terms of incurring interest! If you don't have the cash to buy it, then you can't afford it.

Long-Term Planning

Having a vision for your wardrobe and plan to achieve that vision may sound a little silly. Nevertheless, you'll end up saving a lot of money now and in the long run when you make a plan for what you wear. Some people are creative and like expressing that through their clothing. You can still be creative and save money.

o **Wardrobe planning**

Planning does not have to be boring. In fact, if you're the creative type, challenge yourself to find fewer pieces to mix and match when making different outfits. Matchy-matchy is no longer in fashion. If you take your clothes out of the closet and pile them up, you can probably find several yards of fabric, giving you many options to mix. If you have business suits that you no longer wear, you can break them up into individual pieces and wear them with different items.

If you don't want to express your creativity through your clothes—and there are people who don't—you can consider a uniform. Think about Steve Jobs's iconic black turtleneck; he didn't spend a lot of time dressing in the morning because he always knew what he was going to wear. You may not want to wear a black turtleneck everyday yourself, but maybe your "uniform" is a pair of black pants and a collared shirt in colors you like to wear. Choose what you feel comfortable in.

Having neutrals such as navy, black, and camel in your wardrobe means that you don't have to buy as many clothes. Use them as your staples, and no one will know that you're wearing your black pants twice in one week. Who can tell?

Think *capsule collection*, which is just a term for basics that are timeless. You can mix in accessories and more seasonal pieces as you feel the need to be more creative. However, the backbone of your wardrobe will never go out of style.

o **Reassess stores: think consignments, thrifts, and renting special occasion**

Where are you buying your clothes? You don't necessarily need to go to the mall—consignment and thrifts stores are more likely to have classic pieces by manufacturers that are not designed to fall apart after a few months. They're also great places to shop for your basics, along with some more creative options. The clothes may not be this season's fashion, but you shouldn't worry too much about that. You can gain your own creative style through it or base your wardrobe on timeless classics. Neither of these options are subject to the whims of fashion. Designer clothing can be extremely well-made. Though you may spend more at a consignment store, if you take care of your item, it can last forever.

The trick to thrift and consignment stores is their location. People tend to donate clothes locally, so if you live on the less expensive end of town, you may not find a lot of quality clothing in your thrift store. Therefore, you will need to dig for it. If you travel toward a wealthier section of town, you'll probably find a bigger selection of high-quality clothing. You may find higher price tags, but it'll still be cheaper than buying new.

Direct purchases from China will also often be the cheapest. They do not have seasons for two reasons—first, they sell globally, since spring in North America is autumn in Australia. Second, you pay for production and shipping costs without expensive intermediators.

When it comes to special occasions, such as white or black tie events, consider renting your wardrobe rather than buying it. Women will often only wear dresses for these events once, and the dresses are not cheap. Likewise, men who often attend black-tie events might buy theirs because they may have more use for their suits. Decide if you should be renting or buying, and you will save a lot of money.

- **List anything that's missing from your wardrobe and plan to purchase only that item**

  Once you have your wardrobe plan, you will know if you're missing anything. For example, you might need a coat or blazer if you don't already have one. Since you're planning ahead, you're giving yourself time. Thus, it is time to check the thrift shops and see if they have what you need. Look at coupons and sales for higher quality items and pounce if you find a good price.

  Having a list prevents you from buying things you don't need and mindlessly spending. When you go to the store, you're laser-focused on one specific item; if the item you need isn't there, make a quick exit and go on to the next store.

- **If something comes in, something has to go out**

  Not only will this rule help you declutter your closet, but it will also help you be mindful about your spending. You might end up shopping and browsing through the store and find something that you don't really need or that doesn't fit with your plan. Before purchase, ask yourself what you would get rid of if you bought this item. Doing so gives you the space you need to be mindful about the potential purchase. Do you really need this item? If you don't think you can replace anything with it, you might not need it.

  In another scenario, maybe earlier you bought something intentionally that just didn't quite work out. Perhaps the fabric was too scratchy, or you kept tugging at the lapel. The one-in-one-out rule will help you get rid of it instead of letting it clutter your closet, thus you can replace it with an item that fits your lifestyle better.

Chapter Summary

- You don't have to spend too much money to have a great wardrobe.
- Implement a buy-nothing plan right away and use your time during this pandemic to make any needed repairs.
- In the next few months, have swaps with friends or pick up items you need at a yard sale.
- Plan ahead for your wardrobe and shop only to fill in the gaps in the future.
- Create your own style.

In the next chapter, we will go over some tips for traveling on a budget that will still allow you to enjoy that trip!

SAVE
MONEY
AND
SPEND
WISELY

Chapter EIGHT

TRAVEL TIGHT

RIGHT now, you might not even be thinking about traveling! By contrast, you could be dreaming about taking a vacation once the pandemic is over. The good news is that you can still have an enjoyable trip even while watching your money. There's a lot of information about how to plan and execute a frugal yet wonderful vacation, and now is a great time to start dreaming and planning for a terrific trip.

Quick Tips to Start Now

What kind of trip are you planning to take? There are tons of things you can do, including sightseeing, doing physical activities, and relaxing on the beach. What sounds good to you?

○ **Consider switching to travel rewards credit cards**

The vast majority of credit and debit cards offer some kind of reward. Do you know what kind of rewards yours have? Do some research on your credit or debit card's company to see the kinds of bonus offers your cards give you. If your cards don't include travel rewards, consider switching to ones that do. Go online to find a card that offers good travel rewards and has a low or nonexistent annual fee—preferably zero!

A no-fee credit card won't give you concierge perks, but that's not what you're looking for. You're looking for one that offers good travel rewards, so don't let yourself get sidetracked with "deals" that aren't meaningful to you.

○ **Plan ahead of time & savor the anticipation**

Do you know why now is the perfect time to start planning? It turns out that the biggest pleasure in traveling is actually the anticipation (Andrews, 2018).[18] Studies have found that we're happiest leading up to an event. On some occasions, we are happier than we are during the event, and usually when looking back on it.

With all this free time now, you can start dreaming and thinking about your next event. Savor that anticipation and use this early start to start planning. You'll have a better idea of what you're looking for and can keep an eye out for money-saving opportunities that may arise.

Medium-Term to Implement in the Next Few Months

This is the time to dive into research and planning, now you have a good idea of what you would like to do and what would be best for you.

- **Research**

  Planning is part of the fun and anticipation, and you can save a lot of money doing it! Once you've figured out where you want to go, look into attractions you can visit. If you can, find some free and low-cost activities. Remember from a previous chapter that some museums have free days, so you can add those attractions to your itinerary. There may also be some free festivals or holiday extravaganzas. What looks interesting, fun, and different? Are there any free or low-cost ways for you to take advantage of them? Make sure you include those considerations in your trip.

  A great way to save money is to go during the off-season. Everyone goes to New York during Christmas, which is both expensive and crowded. Therefore, find a different season to go. Likewise, make sure that the attractions you want to visit will be open during the time you go. For example, August in Paris is off-season, but everyone's on vacation for the month, meaning nothing will be open.

  Although exchange rates vary throughout the year and you don't have a lot of control over them, try to take them into account when planning. If the rate is bad for a certain country, you may want to postpone your trip until it becomes a bit more favorable.

- **Use coupons, deals, loyalty programs, and credit card rewards**

  If you travel a lot for business and have gained many points with airlines or chains, use those for your vacation. If you can find deals and coupons for your intended destination, use those too. Hopefully, you can also implement some credit card rewards now too!

  I have used these tricks myself; I traveled to Macchu Picchu in Peru using credit card rewards and airline miles once. I used a low-cost outfitter and shared a tent on the trail. The group I went with all became good friends after one week together, and we learned so much by having a native guide for the trip. I could have spent a lot more money and stayed in more luxurious surroundings, but my more frugal methods led to one of the most memorable trips I'd ever taken. Similarly, I took a service trip with the Sierra Club. My group did some physical work in the park, and I learned a lot and paid *much* less than if I'd gone with a tour group.

So, get creative! That's how you get memorable trips.

- **Be open to change if it's cheaper**

  Flexibility is the key to cheap travel; for example, the airline cost might be significantly less if you leave or return on a different day, or use a different airport. You could also opt to make some slight changes to your itinerary if some other money-saving opportunity arises. Keep an eye out for last-minute deals to your destination.

  However, you'll want to stick with one airline and its business partners; otherwise, you might miss your connection if you come in late and communication between the flights is spotty.

- **Avoid package deals if you don't plan to take advantage of part of the package**

  Cruise lines may offer very luxurious packages, along with some all-inclusive resorts. However, if you don't take advantage of everything they offer, the ideal may not turn out to be so wonderful after all.

  For example, suppose you don't drink alcohol. Does it make sense to go to an all-inclusive resort where one of the biggest benefits is all-you-can-drink alcohol? That is the same on a cruise line. If you're not a very active person, does it make sense to travel on a huge ship where the biggest attraction is the variety of physical activities contained in the offer? Probably not. 257

- **Explore locally**

  Have you explored your area much? Rather than flying or cruis-ing—both of which are pretty bad for the environment—consider driving somewhere near you. Most states have some nice parks that you may have yet to visit or have only visited a part of.

  What nearby attractions have you seen but never been to? Are there any interesting festivals that you could check out within a day's drive or so? Members of AAA receive a monthly maga-zine that lists interesting events happening nearby, and you can also check out events online.

  Maybe you can't afford a big trip every year. Nevertheless, that doesn't mean you can't have a little vacation more often. Use your vacation days and take an interesting and fun break more often and when you can't take a big one.

- **Consider more interesting accommodations**

  Hotels can be expensive—fortunately, there exist many other less expensive options! Bed and breakfasts, short-term rentals, hos-tels, and even swapping your home with someone else can all be cheaper and more fun options than a boring corporate hotel.

  Make sure you open up your search to include non-hotel op-tions. As a bonus, you will have the opportunity to see non-touristy places and how the locals live, or try some unique food.

Long-Term Planning

Great—now that you've done all your research, what's next?

- **Save up**

  Do you have enough cash saved to finance your trip? If not, you can't afford that trip. This doesn't mean, however, that you have to pay for everything in cash! It just means that you may want to wait a little longer before you take that vacation.

258

The savings you've been making along the way in your budget should help. You just don't want to put your trip on your credit card, then be unable to pay it off when you get back.

- **Be smart when you reach your destination**

  Rather than eating out at restaurants all the time, go grocery shopping for food. The bonus will be that you get to meet local people and not just other tourists eating in the restaurants. You may also get to eat what the locals do.

  You'll probably want to bring home some souvenirs that will remind you of your lovely trip, but don't overspend. Buy something that's meaningful from the place you're visiting and that fits your budget—not the cheapest junk in the shop or something you can get at home.

  I had a friend who loved jewelry, and she would always buy a pair of earrings from the street vendors when she traveled. When she got home, no one else was wearing the same thing.

- **Budget for a splurge or two, but not the whole time**

  When you're in Paris, you will obviously go to eat at a romantic restaurant. Likewise, you will probably go to a Broadway show when you're in New York (with half-price tickets if you buy the day of the show) or visit the beer garden in certain areas of Germany.

  Don't splurge every day, but when you do decide to splurge, enjoy it! It's a treat.

- **Find a vacation that combines two concepts**

  You want to relax on the beach, but you also want to do some fun activities; therefore, find a spot where you can do both. You may need to drive a bit to reach your second destination, but it'll be worth it.

Chapter Summary

- Travel and fun do not have to be expensive.
- Start dreaming and planning now because anticipation is the best part of the trip!
- In the next few months, do your research and plan a wonderful and inexpensive trip, which doesn't have to be overseas.
- On your trip, you can plan for a splurge or two, but be smart at your destination.

In the next chapter, we will discuss how to create a wonderful and inexpensive future today.

[18] https://www.nathab.com/blog/anticipation-is-the-happiest-part-of-a-travel-journey/

Chapter NINE

CREATE YOUR FUTURE TODAY

NOW it's time to put everything together! There are a lot of ways to save money that we've listed in this book, and it's OK if you're feeling a little overwhelmed! Maybe you've seen some of the information before, though much of it is still new. If you haven't started your journey yet, here's how you can finally put your plan into action.

Remember to take deep breaths and let your reasoning brain take over! Money and finances often make people stress out, so make sure you're calm and not feeling too anxious. Taking action makes your brain happy, and planning is the first step to take. Here's how you can really make a difference in saving your money.

The following ten steps will change your life, so read through them first to see how the system works. Then, come on back and start taking action on step one. Once you decide to put these into place, you'll start saving money. Reading is great, but the only way you can make big changes is by taking action!

1. Determine where you are now

Choose a free expense-tracking app and get started. They're all pretty much the same, so don't spend a lot of time picking one. The apps can't necessarily go back in time and pick up earlier spending, so this is where some homework comes in.

Gather up your credit and debit card statements, your checking statement, and receipts—a spreadsheet is probably the easiest way to enter all these expenses. Hopefully, you can export everything from your credit card companies, so then you can copy and paste those into the spreadsheet. Categorize the spending if it's not already done for you: groceries, entertainment, car, etc. You can then choose categories from chapters 2-8 or your own, whichever you prefer.

Having three months is best. That way, you can average them out, as one month might be especially high or low for a specific reason. Averaging the three months gives you a pretty good estimate of what you're actually spending. Once you've done all that, total the amount you've spent in each category, along with the total for the month.

2. Pick a category to start

This book is organized into the following categories: food, home, wired services, entertainment, vehicles, wardrobe, and travel.

Start with an easy topic, where you know you can make a difference right away by dropping a product or service, or selling something. In some subjects, you may already know where you tend to overspend.

3. Go back to that chapter and read the suggestions

Which of the chapters is applicable to you? For example, in the chapter about your home, there are suggestions for both renters and homeowners. If you own your house, the renter suggestions won't apply to you, and vice versa.

Which ones can you commit to taking right now or within the next one to three months? Are there any long-term ideas that you can commit to or consider right now? Think about these questions.

4. Write down the steps you want to take

You will need to get out a paper and pen for this one. I still write things down, as writing things down helps to clarify and prioritize things for yourself. It will make you feel less anxious because your brain isn't tasked with trying to maintain that note too. Writing rather than typing has been shown to help us both remember and process things better (Doubek, 2016).[19] Therefore, whichever steps you've decided to take, write them down. Another benefit of writing them down is that, when you complete the step, you can cross it off, which is very satisfying.

I created a one page form that will come in handy for tracking every saving, from planning to recording the results, and with instructions for filling out each section. If you have yet to download it, please use the link that you find in the beginning of this book right after the Table of Contents.

Give yourself a deadline for each step. For example, if you want to call your service providers, give yourself three days to do it. Then, put it in your calendar or task list, so you can have a reminder that it's due.

Who else needs to be involved in the step? Do you need some sort of agreement or help from your spouse, like with selling the car? Estimate the savings for these steps.

5. Write SMART goals for longer-term plans

The suggestions for the long term tend to require more planning, or at least more consideration on your part. You can think in terms of SMART goals: Specific, Measurable, Achievable, Relevant and Time-bound.

Maybe you're considering moving. What actions do you need to achieve this goal? You'll need to research your potential location and all associated costs, and calculate your commute fees and wear and tear. When will you have the research done? When will you be able to make the decision? Write down the small steps that will help you reach your goal, then put those into your calendar too.

6. Write down the positive effects of taking these actions

You don't want to feel deprived! In addition, if you keep thinking negatively in terms of what you're cutting back, you will probably feel that way. It may not be a great idea now out of excitement for potential savings, but down the line, consider what it is you're achieving so you can avoid binging and splurging.

Taking action isn't just positive for your wallet, but you'll also get to exercise some creativity, even if you hadn't done so in a while! You may uncover new skills or abilities during this ordeal. How beautiful is it to enjoy the present moment without worrying about whether your car, house, or spouse is as nice as your neighbors or friends? You won't be worrying about having to maintain a standard of living and spending more time with friends and family. You will get to spend your precious time with your loved ones instead of watching TV.

Write down the positive effects, along with the next-order consequences. Now that you're saving more, you can pay off debts, build up an emergency fund, or plan something on your bucket list. Whatever it is, write it down. Really explore the positive changes these savings will make on your life.

7. Take at least one short-term action

You know your brain loves action. Planning is key, but implementing is even more crucial, so start small and pick a quick win. Most of these short-term suggestions don't require too much work or thought.

Once you've taken the action, you may have gained an immediate savings number. For example, if you negotiated a discount on services, you'll be paying some amount less than you were before, which you will want to write down. On the other hand, there is a chance you might have previously thought that you couldn't handle your money. With that thought, you're already taking control. It doesn't have to be hard—although some of these steps may take a little more time, you've just shown yourself that you can do it! Consider sharing your experience with your friends. Not only will doing so reaffirm what you've achieved, but you may also inspire and help them.

8. If you're having trouble, distinguish desire from necessity

People get stuck sometimes, and they're not quite sure what they can do to adjust their lives financially. You might even feel that some of our steps are a bit extreme, even if they aren't. The extreme is, rather, how mindlessly we may spend. Once you prioritize your goal of saving money, you will see how all the ideas make sense.

However, when you do get stuck, go back to the fundamental difference between *want* and *need*. You need nutritious food that provides natural vitamins and minerals, and preferably either protein, fat, or fiber. Does your proposed purchase match this? If it doesn't, don't buy it because it's a want and not a need.

Sometimes, you may have to compromise when you have two conflicting needs, or you prioritize one over the other temporarily. However, most of the time, something you believe is a need really is more of a want. When you delve deep into it, you will realize that.

9. Start on another section and repeat

These techniques can be used for every category in the book! Start small and easy with quick wins you can capture right away. Doing so makes it easier in the long haul, and you will be able to say to yourself that you can do this, as you'll have proof that you can save money. Then, it's just a matter of figuring out how to do it.

10. Reflect on how much you saved

You should have some actual earnings from the quick tips you implemented, including calling service providers and selling anything you no longer need. Add up your savings and feel proud of how much you've done.

You still have plenty more to go with long-term decisions that will give you more for your money. Don't forget the smaller ones add up too.

Do you feel deprived? Or do you feel more connected, more creative, and on a more solid foundation? I bet that you're feeling pretty good right about now!

SAVE
MONEY
AND
SPEND
WISELY

Chapter Summary

- There are a lot of ways to save money, and, although it may feel overwhelming, you can create a plan that can put all these savings in place for you.
- Start tracking your spending and determine where you are right now.
- Take one category and write down the actions you plan to take, including long-term goals.
- Pick an easy way to save money and do it!
- Continue with the other categories, implementing and calculating your savings as you go.

In the next chapter, we will go over how to stay motivated and continue saving in the future

---

[19] https://www.npr.org/2016/04/17/474525392/attention-students-put-your-laptops-away

Chapter TEN

CONTINUE SAVING

IF you implemented just a few of the suggestions from this book so far, you've already saved money and are hopefully on the path to high-quality entertainment and time with family and friends. Now comes the challenging part: maintaining your new habits. Having to stay home during the crisis may have made it easier to avoid shopping and spending. However, you have made some big, positive changes that you should continue for a happier life with less spending.

Evaluate

First, take a look at what you've done so far. How much money have you saved tangibly, like in phone savings or avoiding new purchases? How much of that can you attribute to staying home due to the coronavirus? For example, suppose you normally like to window shop, and you end up buying things you don't really need. Having the stores closed means you've probably saved a lot of money because you couldn't do that. On the other hand, the lower prices you negotiated for services and the things you sold are not necessarily due to the epidemic.

Will you have difficulty not shopping once you can head to the mall again? The answer to this question is why you wrote down all the positive benefits to your new habits. It's not just about the money, but the time you have not worrying about that money. Along with that, it's also about the time you're spending with friends at the park or at their houses.

When you feel the itch to go shopping, turn back and read all those positive changes you wrote about that happened as a result of not shopping and saving your money instead. Do you want to jeopardize that? If you absolutely must go browsing, use the leave-your-wallet-behind trick we discussed, so you don't actually end up spending money.

You know by now that, when you do something pleasurable, your brain releases the feel-good neurotransmitter dopamine. In other words, your brain is saying, yes, let's do that again! Often, people get that little hit when they buy something. This dopamine hit is temporary and wears off fast. The pleasure in that purchase will probably dissipate before you even get your items to the car or see the purchase on your credit card statement.

Humans are adaptable creatures, and we adjust to new lifestyles pretty quickly. Things that originally brought us a lot of pleasure will eventually subside; for example, once most people get a raise, they will increase their spending to adjust to the new income instead of saving it. That new, shiny car is exciting when you can first afford it, but it will feel like nothing special after a while. You may have heard this referred to as the hedonic treadmill (in which "hedonic" refers to "pleasure") (Pennock, 2019).[20]

Once you get on this treadmill, it's hard to get off! That's when you're most susceptible to ads that suggest you'll be healthier, 271 happier, or richer if you buy their product or service. One of the best ways to avoid or get off of this treadmill is to find meaning and purpose in your life. That's right—all the work you've been doing to develop new skills and spend more time with people will also help you avoid the need to buy for pleasure. Exercise, which you've probably started doing, is also a source of pleasure.

You can add that to your list of positive benefits too—that your new life, free of spending, is making you happier than your old one in which you spent too much money out of habit. If you feel like a rebel, this is an excellent way to rebel: spending more time and money on your loved ones, and less on big corporations!

Maintain Motivation

The silver lining to the crisis is that it made most of us do things differently. If you had bad habits, like hitting the coffee shop or cardboard masquerading as a sweet treat, you've been forced to break that habit. If you wandered aimlessly around the mall every Saturday morning, you've broken that habit.

Leave those habits broken—there is no need to race out once the restrictions are lifted and spend money just because you can. By now, you should have developed the habit of thinking mindfully about your expenses. Do you need or want it? If it's a want, then you probably don't need to spend money on it.

Having goals becomes more important when we can get back out there and hit the mall or the electronics store. You're not saving money just because someone told you to or financial planners say it's a good idea. If your only reason for saving money is because someone else thinks you should, there's no way you can stop spending too much over the long term.

You might be riding high on the idea of savings in the immediate
future; at some point, however, you will see something you want.

Not something you need, but something that you want. When that happens, if the only thing standing between you and that purchase is how someone else told you that not spending is a good idea, you will spend like it's your last day on Earth.

However, now you're armed with your goals. You know you don't have infinite time or billions of dollars to spend and need to prioritize. It may be tempting, but you need your home and to save for that down payment. You could be paying off your credit cards or building up your emergency fund. In this case, you also would no longer be living paycheck to paycheck.

Plus, look at all the great things you did when you saved money. Your loved ones can be lots of fun! You discovered that you're really good at playing guitar, even though you haven't done it since seventh grade. You and your friends hang out after the weekly match to have fun. You're no longer a spender—you've evolved, even over this relatively short time. Your priorities have focused more on what's good for you rather than on material items. Now, you're the person who has control over their money, rather than letting their money take control of them, which is pretty cool. You're smart about your money, and you think about where you want to use them.

None of this means that you'll never spend again! Of course, you have the needs that you must satisfy, along with people to hang out with and new things to do. Some of these needs will require careful and mindful spending. If you've rediscovered playing the guitar, you might need to invest a bit in your guitar and maybe some lessons. Whatever your new hobby or craft is, you'll probably need to acquire some tools and/or materials to continue with it. This is all how you should think about your expenses going forward. What serves you and your goals? If a purchase doesn't satisfy one of these two items, you shouldn't buy it.

Future

There are some goals that you need to have for your savings and to make sure that you don't end up in a lot of credit card debt.

○ **Pay off credit card debt**

Interest compounding against you can make it hard to get out of your hole of debt once you're in it. The first thing to do, of course, is to not add any more debt to your cards. Save up for big purchases, so even if you do put them on the card to attain rewards points, you can pay them off immediately and not accrue interest.

Most of the time, minimum payments don't cut it, and you will need to add a little extra to one card until you've paid it off. Then, add that amount to the monthly payments on the nest card until it's paid off. You'll also pay that card off faster if you tackle your high-interest card first. However, if you're easily discouraged, pick one with a small balance that you can pay off faster, then get the quick win that will motivate you to continue.

○ **Emergency fund**

You need three to six months' worth of expenses in cash to take care of any emergency that might arise. It's a little late for the coronavirus, but you can insulate yourself from a job layoff or other problem in the future by having this cash stashed away. A little is better than none, so put a small amount away and save more when you can.

○ **Retirement**

Very few workers have access to pensions anymore, so most of us will be retiring on whatever's left of Social Security and what we have saved. Therefore, you need to save! The earlier you start, the better.

Recall the Rule of 72—your portfolio doubles every 12 years if you earn 6% on average, which is a reasonable portfolio return. If you only have twelve years to save, you will only have one double. So, you would either have to save a massive amount each year over the next 12 years, or have far less money available. If you start saving in your forties and have 24 years to retirement, you will have two doubles. Likewise, if you start in your twenties, you will have at least three doubles.

Suggest that you start with $10,000, ignoring additions that will also increase the amount. Starting in your fifties: one double, $20,000. Starting in your forties: two doubles, $40,000. But in your twenties? Starting with $10,000, you will end up with $80,000 by doing nothing except investing the money and leaving it alone.

Chapter Summary

- Evaluate how much you've saved so far.
- Be mindful of your goals and what you value to keep your new saving and spending habits, even when the restrictions are over.
- Other goals for saving should include a payment of all credit card debt, creation of an emergency fund, and retirement.
- Remember that today, you are creating your future!

---

[20] https://positivepsychology.com/hedonic-treadmill/

SAVE MONEY AND SPEND WISELY

FINAL WORDS

WE'VE pooled various suggestions and ways to plan your savings in this book. Thus, it's important for you to continue your good money habits, even after the crisis is over. When people are back to work earning a salary and shops are open, it will be more tempting to spend money.

However, now you are in control of your money. If you started the book without a good foundation for handling your finances, now you have a strong one and know that that's key to managing your spending. It shouldn't be because someone told you to, but because, after implementing these ideas and seeing your savings grow, you know that it puts you on the path to achieving your goals. You also now recognize that money is a tool and nothing more. It's not how much you're worth as a person, and it doesn't signify how valuable you are.

After reading the book, you've gained a better grasp of how the human brain works, especially when it comes to your personal finances. When your brain feels threatened, it sets your fight-or-flight response into action, which is great for running away from the lion that's about to eat you. It is not, however, so great at making financial decisions. You've also gained some techniques for bringing your rational brain back online, so you can make better decisions by reasoning through them. You can now balance the short-term pleasure of spending with the long-term need to save and reach your goals.

A key factor in keeping your spending reasonable is to distinguish between what you want and what you need. It's necessary to spend money on necessities like shelter, food, and clothing, but you don't have to overspend, and there are numerous ways to bring various costs down.

None of us have infinite amounts of money or time, so we have to prioritize. And this is good; otherwise, we would be spending our entire lives buying things. We each have to consider our values and spend according to that. Yet, there is still no need to spend mindlessly on what's of value! For example, many of us enjoy being with our friends. However, you can hang out with your friends at other places besides the bar or expensive pro sports games. You can simply go to the park or someone's house, with a potluck and BYOB. If you and your friends love sports, most communities have amateur sports that you can watch, which are often cheaper and nostalgic. Even better would be playing a sport in a rec league or some kind of community team.

Most people also have financial goals they want to achieve, like buying a house or having a good retirement. It's good to have these in mind and written down in front of you. When you're tempted, these goals will help you remember why you're saving in the first place, making it easier to avoid falling for a gimmick.

Thinking about each purchase and coming up with creative alternatives instead of defaulting to buying things aren't just excellent ways to save lots of money, but they are also good for your mental and physical health. Being with friends and family instead of screens and expensive gadgets satisfies the basic need for human connection. Playing with your kids, pets, or friends also provides exercise that you can enjoy. In addition, it can help to be mindful about your expenses, when watching your mindfulness in other areas.

These are some of the intangible benefits of implementing the ideas from this book, but there are tangible ones too! Even small monthly savings add up significantly over time. We covered the main areas of spending for most people: food, home, cell/Internet services, entertainment, cars, clothing, and travel, and you found strategies that you can use right now, during the coronavirus pandemic. Some strategies include calling your service providers to reduce rates, shopping in your own pantry, and using cookbooks or the internet to find recipes for whatever's been hiding at the back of your cupboard.

We also provided suggestions that may take a little bit more planning or waiting on for when the country is no longer social distancing. These are the medium-term solutions, such as ordering appetizers, splitting entrees when going out to eat, or checking out yard sales if you need an item for your wardrobe.

Long-term tips in each chapter typically require even more planning. For example, you might rethink where you're living if you have a large house and long commute to work. Big houses also have big maintenance and utility bills, and long commutes don't just add wear and tear to the car, but also affect your and your family's mental health. Figuring out alternatives for that will take some research and hard conversations about what's livable and what's reasonable.

You've also learned to keep track of your expenses with free apps available online. Although old school methods included keeping receipts and spreadsheets, you should now be able to see exactly where your money goes. More importantly, you can see how much you're saving as a result of the tips you've learned from this book!

Saving and mindful spending are great techniques you can deploy over your entire life. As circumstances change, you can then have the flexibility to adapt. You might learn some new tips or find new ways to be creative with that which is important to you. Continuing to learn new things is also crucial for your mental health and growth.

The benefits of controlling your money aren't just financial—they extend to all the areas of your life. Thus, happy saving!

SAVE MONEY AND SPEND WISELY

Resources

A. *(2020, January 17).* **Are Social Media and Depression Linked | Florida Behavioral Health Center.** *Retrieved March 25, 2020, from https://www.bhpalmbeach.com/are-depression-and-social-media-usage-linked/*

Andrews, C. G. *(2019, December 31).* **Anticipation Is the Happiest Part of a Travel Journey.** *Retrieved March 28, 2020, from https://www.nathab.com/blog/anticipation-is-the-happiest-part-of-a-travel-journey/*

A.P.T. | . *(2017, February 20).* **8 Powerful Benefits of Writing Things Down.** *Retrieved March 28, 2020, from https://www.productiveandfree.com/blog/writing-things-down-benefits*

Bradford, A. *(2017, March 7).* **Dishwasher vs. hand-washing: What saves more water?** *Retrieved March 25, 2020, from https://www.cnet.com/how-to/how-much-water-do-dishwashers-use/*

Carinsurance.com. *(2012, July 27).* **Don't Insure an Old Car Like a New One.** *Retrieved March 25, 2020, from https://www.nasdaq.com/articles/dont-insure-an-old-car-like-a-new-one-2012-07-27*

Carney PHC. *(2019, February 14).* **Using Those Ceiling Fans to Help Heat Your Home.** *Retrieved March 25, 2020, from https://www.carneyphc.com/blog/heating/using-ceiling-fans-help-heat-home/*

Crank, J. *(2019, November 12).* **How Much Can You Save By Adjusting Your Thermostat?** *Retrieved March 25, 2020, from https://www.directenergy.com/blog/how-much-can-you-save-by-adjusting-your-thermostat/*

Department of Health & Human Services. *(2016, August 10).* **The dangers of sitting: why sitting is the new smoking.** *Retrieved March 25, 2020, from https://www.betterhealth.vic.gov.au/health/healthyliving/the-dangers-of-sitting*

Doubek, J. *(2016, April 17).* **Attention Students: Put Your Laptops Away.** *Retrieved March 28, 2020, from https://choice.npr.org/index.html?origin=https://www.npr.org/2016/04/17/474525392/attention-students-put-your-laptops-away*

Duke, A. *(2018).* **Thinking in Bets.** Zaltbommel, Netherlands: Van Haren Publishing.

Elkins, K. *(2019, October 18).* **Economists say this is the minimum amount of money you need in an emergency fund.** *Retrieved March 25, 2020, from https://www.cnbc.com/2019/10/18/minimum-amount-of-money-you-need-in-an-emergency-fund.html*

Finke, M. *(2016, January 21).* **Old Age and the Decline in Financial Literacy.** *Retrieved March 25, 2020, from https://pubsonline.informs.org/doi/10.1287/mnsc.2015.2293*

Goleman, D. *(2009).* **Emotional Intelligence.** Zaltbommel, Netherlands: Van Haren Publishing.

Gu, K. *(2019, July 3).* **Can People Send and Receive Text Messages via VoIP?** *Retrieved March 25, 2020, from https://www.genvoice.net/can-people-send-and-receive-text-messages-via-voip/*

Hunt, M. *(2016, July 14).* **Wash Clothes Inside Out and Other Laundry Tips and Tricks.** *Retrieved March 28, 2020, from https://www.creators.com/read/everyday-cheapskate/07/16/wash-clothes-inside-out-and-other-laundry-tips-and-tricks*

IRS. *(n.d.).* **Standard Mileage Rates | Internal Revenue Service.** *Retrieved March 25, 2020, from https://www.irs.gov/tax-professionals/standard-mileage-rates*

Kahneman, D. *(2011).* **Thinking, Fast and Slow.** Amsterdam, Netherlands: Adfo Books.

LaPonsie, M. *(2019, August 5).* **Best 5 Expense Tracker Apps.** *Retrieved March 25, 2020, from https://money.usnews.com/money/personal-finance/saving-and-budgeting/articles/best-expense-tracker-apps*

Mcleod, S. *(2020, March 20).* **Maslow's Hierarchy of Needs.** *Retrieved March 25, 2020, from https://www.simplypsychology.org/maslow.html*

Nottingham, P. *(2017, March 15)*. Your Business's Videos Should Include Faces. Here's Why. *Retrieved March 25, 2020, from https://wistia.com/learn/marketing/power-of-faces-in-video*

Pennock, S. *(2019, February 11)*. The Hedonic Treadmill - Are We Forever Chasing Rainbows? *Retrieved March 28, 2020, from https://positivepsychology.com/hedonic-treadmill/*

Price, C. *(2019, February 21)*. Trapped - the secret ways social media is built to be addictive (and what you can do to fight back). *Retrieved March 25, 2020, from https://www.sciencefocus.com/future-technology/trapped-the-secret-ways-social-media-is-built-to-be-addictive-and-what-you-can-do-to-fight-back/*

Sitlers. *(2019, November 4)*. Choose the Right LED Color Temperature for You! . *Retrieved March 25, 2020, from https://sitlersledsupplies.com/choose-right-led-color-temperature/*

Stahl, A. *(2018, August 12)*. Here's How Creativity Actually Improves Your Health. *Retrieved March 25, 2020, from https://www.forbes.com/sites/ashleystahl/2018/07/25/heres-how-creativity-actually-improves-your-health/#18d6ba0913a6*

Swartz, A. *(2020, January 7)*. What happens at the end of a car lease. *Retrieved March 25, 2020, from https://www.policygenius.com/loans/what-happens-at-the-end-of-a-car-lease/*

Upwork. *(2019, November 15)*. Sixth annual "Freelancing in America" study finds that more people than ever see freelancing as a long-term career path. *Retrieved March 28, 2020, from https://www.upwork.com/press/2019/10/03/freelancing-in-america-2019/*

US Dep't of Energy. *(n.d.)*. Gas Saving Tips. *Retrieved March 25, 2020, from https://afdc.energy.gov/files/u/publication/gas-saving_tips_july_2013.pdf*

US Dep't of Energy. *(n.d.)*. Lighting Controls. *Retrieved March 25, 2020, from https://www.energy.gov/energysaver/save-electricity-and-fuel/lighting-choices-save-you-money/lighting-controls*

Viscera. *(2017, March 16)*. Minimalism Series: What's a Capsule Collection? *Retrieved March 28, 2020, from https://shopviscera.com/blogs/happenings/minimalism-series-whats-a-capsule-collection*

Leave a Review

I would be incredibly *thankful* if you could take just 60 seconds to write a brief review on Amazon, even if it's just a few sentences.

If you have downloaded the checklist with top ten tips for your daily productivity and/or the one page form for tracking your savings (the link is at the beginning of the book), you can take a photo, attach it to the review and share your experience. Your success will inspire and encourage many readers who may be struggling in the beginning.

Please log into your Amazon account, then find this book *2-in-1 Value Bundle: Save Money and Work from Home During and After the Economic Crisis.*

Alternatively type this link into your browser or scan the QR code:
amazon.com/dp/B08MN8W7L2

Customer Reviews

★ ★ ★ ★ ★ 51

4.8 out of 5 stars ▾

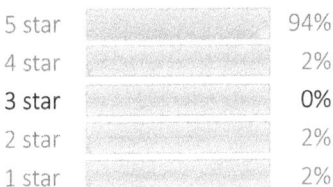

5 star		94%
4 star		2%
3 star		0%
2 star		2%
1 star		2%

Share your thoughts with other customers

Write a customer review

See all 51 customer reviews ▸

Dana Wise

SAVE MONEY AND WORK FROM HOME
DURING AND AFTER THE ECONOMIC CRISIS

2020

www.ingramcontent.com/pod-product-compliance
Lightning Source LLC
Chambersburg PA
CBHW030456210326
41597CB00013B/690